The Art Of Making Armour

A Craftman's Guide To Creating Authentic Armour Reproductions

Rob Valentine

American Literary Press, Inc.
Five Star Special Edition
Baltimore, Maryland

The Art Of Making Armour

A Craftman's Guide To Creating Authentic Armour Reproductions

Library of Congress
Cataloging in Publication Data
ISBN 1-56167-527-X

Library of Congress Card Catalog Number:
99-63187

Published by

American Literary Press, Inc.
Five Star Special Edition
8019 Belair Road, Suite 10
Baltimore, Maryland 21236

Manufactured in the United States of America

Foreword

I know what attracts me to armour. As an artist, I appreciate its combination of functionality and esthetics. Through study and by making armour for over 17 years, I've watched armour design and function change throughout history. It adapted to new and formidable weapons, and to fashion changes.

Throughout this book, I am using the sixteenth century to explain armouring techniques. It seems to be the most frequently referred to when we envision a "knight in shining armour." It was in this century where full plate armour reached its zenith.

It is important to note that there are very little written accounts by armourers, and virtually no explanation as to how armour was made. One can only surmise it's creation by studying original pieces and pictures of armourers' workshops in contemporary art works, such as paintings, woodcuts, and rare manuscripts. Armourers were protective of their craft, and secretive with their techniques and processes.

Generally, armouring was a family business, where ideas were passed on from father to son. These family secrets were kept for two main reasons: 1) For maintaining high quality techniques to ensure getting contracts from royalty (and preventing the competition getting the contracts). 2) For keeping military secrets (such as alloys mixed with steel or hardening techniques) which was encouraged by loyalties.

Robert Valentine, Owner
Valentine Armouries

Introduction

In this book we will attempt to clarify modern misconceptions about armour, as well as demonstrate different theories on armour construction.

This book shouldn't be considered as a conclusive manual, but rather as an "easy to understand" point of view by Valentine Armouries.

Steel is taken for granted now, whereas the smelting of steel was an expensive process in medieval times. Only noblemen, chivalry, and royalty could afford to commission weapons and armour. The process of making armour would have begun with ingots of steel, hammered into sheets of various thicknesses. The steel used today is of higher quality and has less impurities. The gauges of steel used in authentic armour would have varied from 20 to 16 gauge on "field harnesses." Field harness means it was worn on the battlefield. The average field harness weighed as light as 50 to 70 pounds.

Tournament armour, weighing about 150 pounds, was much heavier because it was reinforced on the front and left side. The thickness of tournament armour could go up to 3/16" thick in high target areas, such as the breastplate, and could vary from 3/16" thick in the centre to 1/8" thin on the extremities, where reinforcement wasn't necessary.

Armour was custom made to fit the buyer, like a set of fine clothes. The armourer was considered a "tailor of steel clothes". This is evident because the design of armour reflected the fashion of clothing of the time.

ARMOUR PARTS:

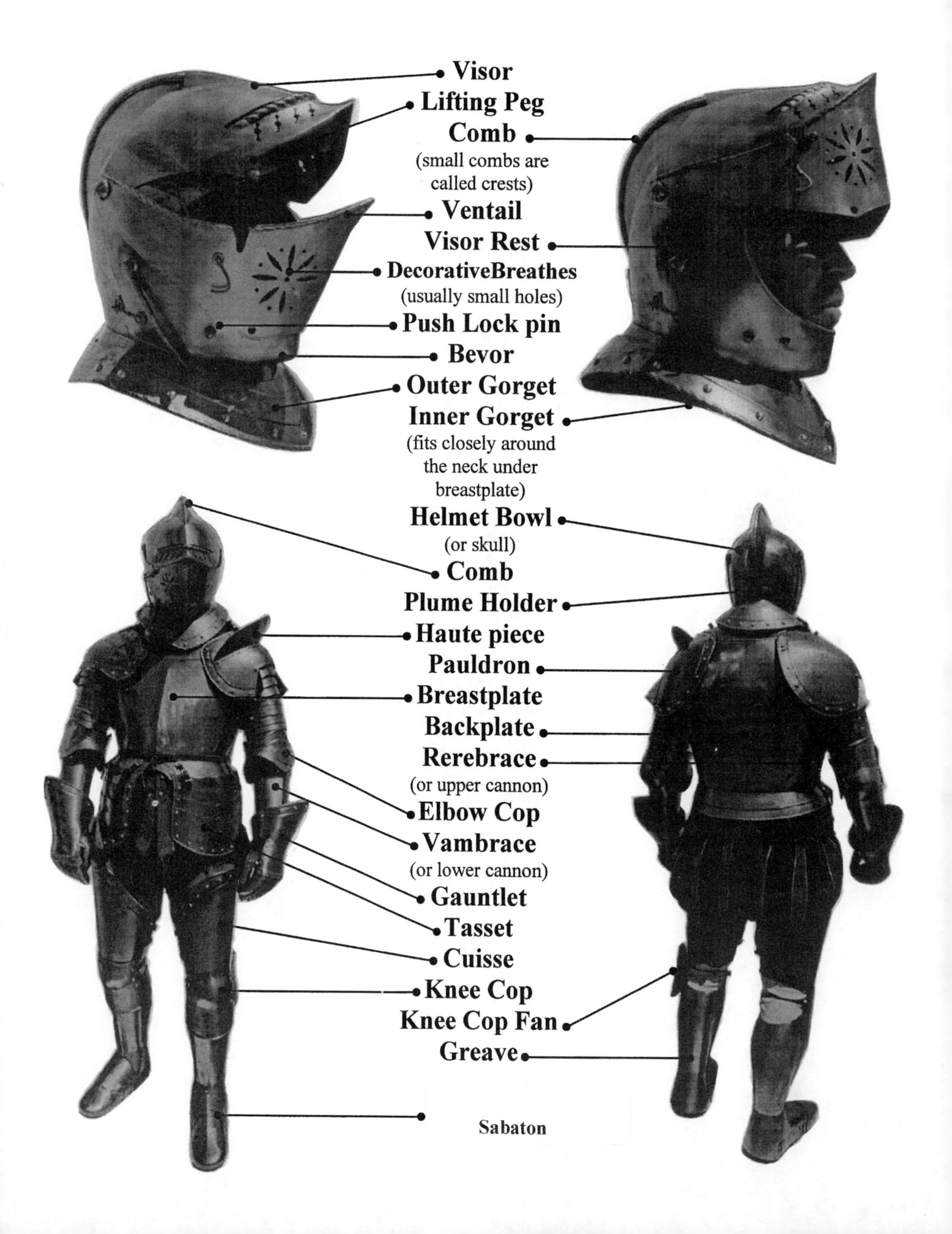

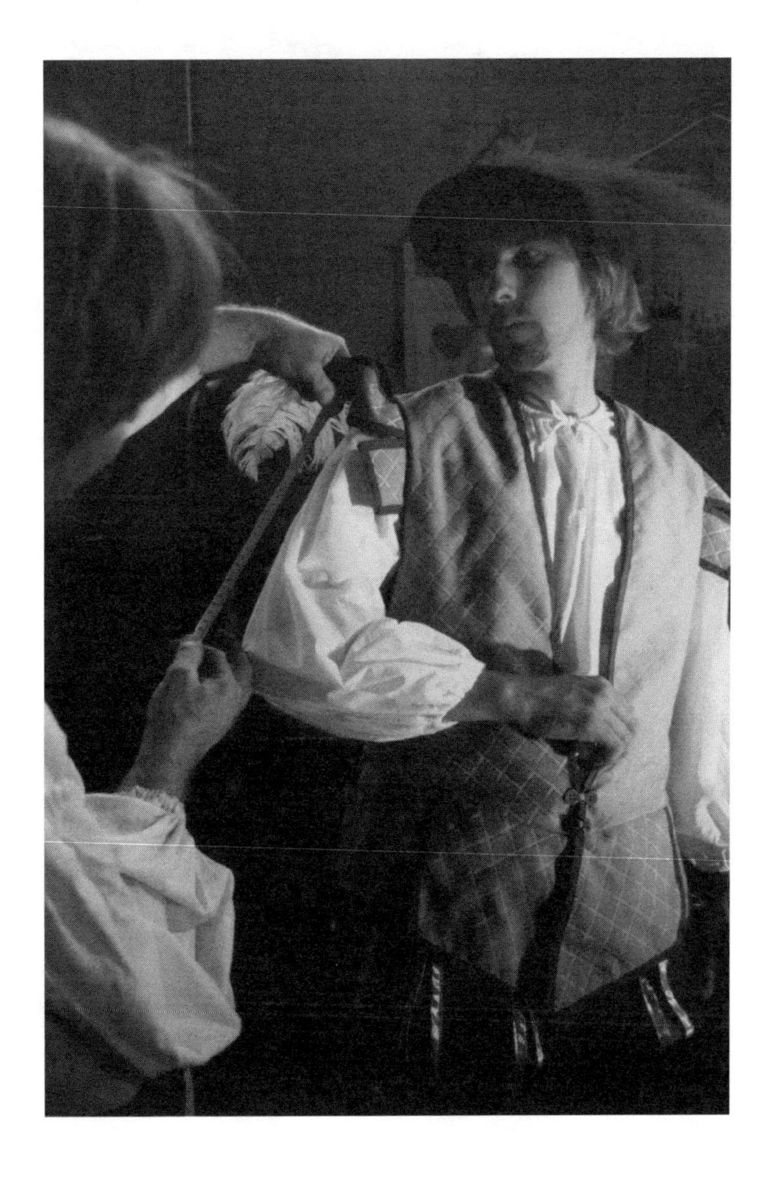

The client is first measured for a suit of armour. The historical armourer would have showed the customer various designs, drawn in a book for him to choose from. Most likely, he would have wanted his suit to be unique, to reflect his needs, tastes, and possibly his beliefs. A religious symbol etched on the breastplate was common at the time.

Most armour was custom made, with the exception of Munition's Armour, made for an average sized foot soldier. These items included arms, morions, kettle hats, and breastplates.

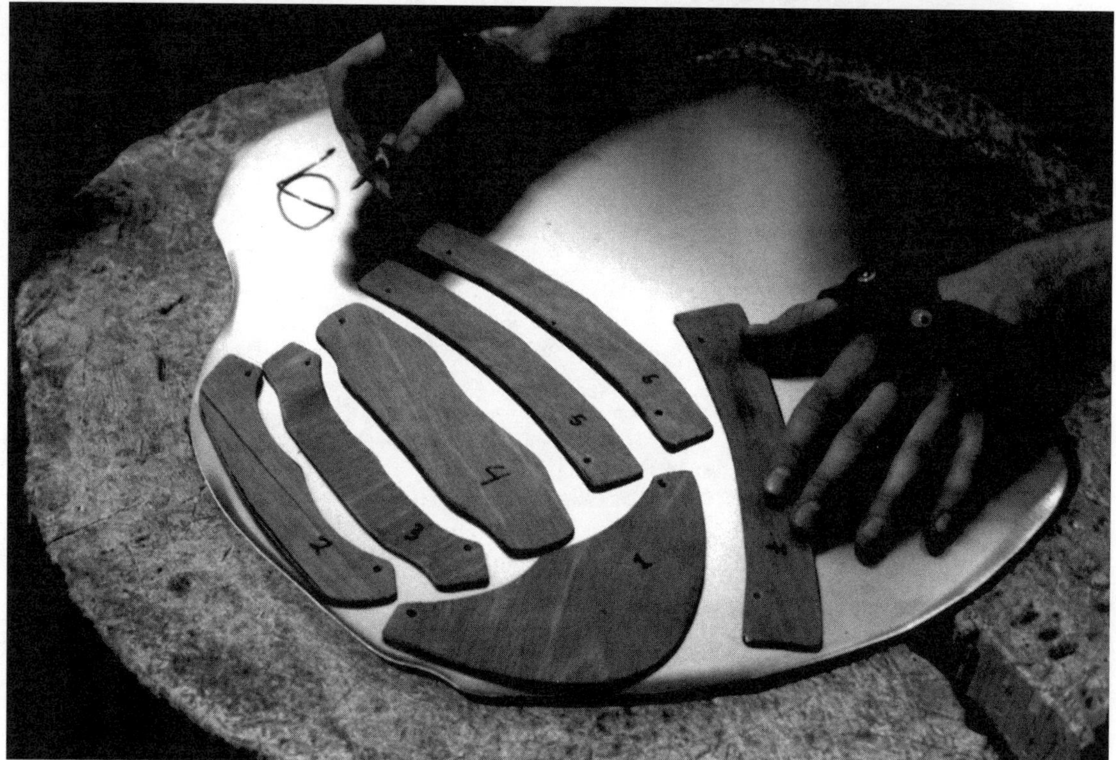

Templates were probably made of wood, as demonstrated here. Adjusting for size, the apprentices would scribe the designs on the appropriate plates of steel.

By the sixteenth century, most of the steel would have been ordered from platers, a separate business outside the armourer's shop. Armourers would order different sizes and thicknesses of steel for their specifications.

Platers and armourers would situate their shops near running water. They needed water for the forging process. As well, they would harness the water with water wheels to run mechanisms with cogs, gears, and belts to power their tools (such as the trip hammer, and the grinding and polishing wheels).

For cutting steel, the armourers would use giant shears affixed to a stump. Using leverage, they would cut the steel down to a more manageable piece. Then they used hand cutters for final cuts. All edges were then hand filed before they were shaped.

The armourer's mark was used to identify who made it, and where.

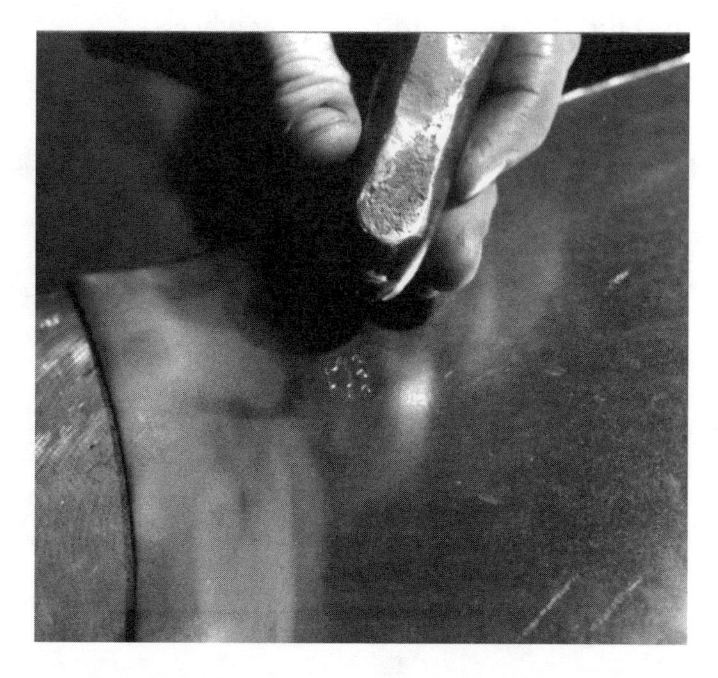

Armour marks would be put on pieces in some cases before stretching, but usually afterwards.

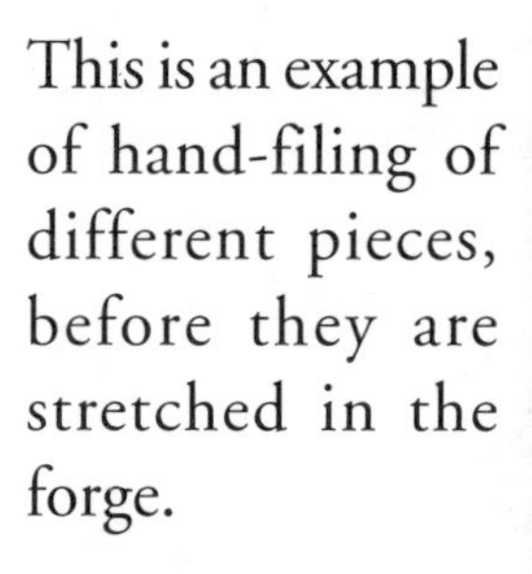

This is an example of hand-filing of different pieces, before they are stretched in the forge.

We will start by showing the forging of the breastplate. Only the thickest pieces need to be heated to be shaped.

This 16 gauge breastplate must be heated to red hot so it can stretch without cracking.

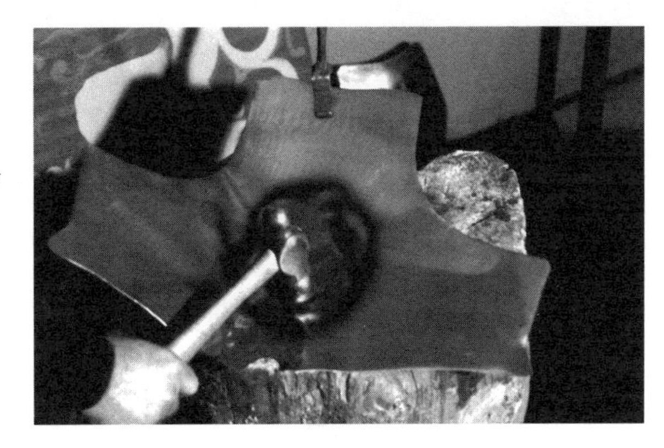

It is stretched by hammering it into a shallow hole in a wood stump.

Several different stretching stumps would have been used for various curves and depths of armour parts. Anvils would have been used to take the wrinkles out of the steel and to clean up the hammer marks.

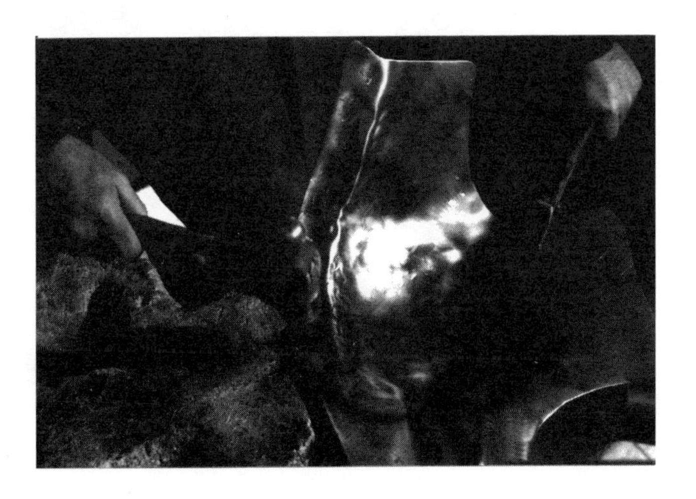

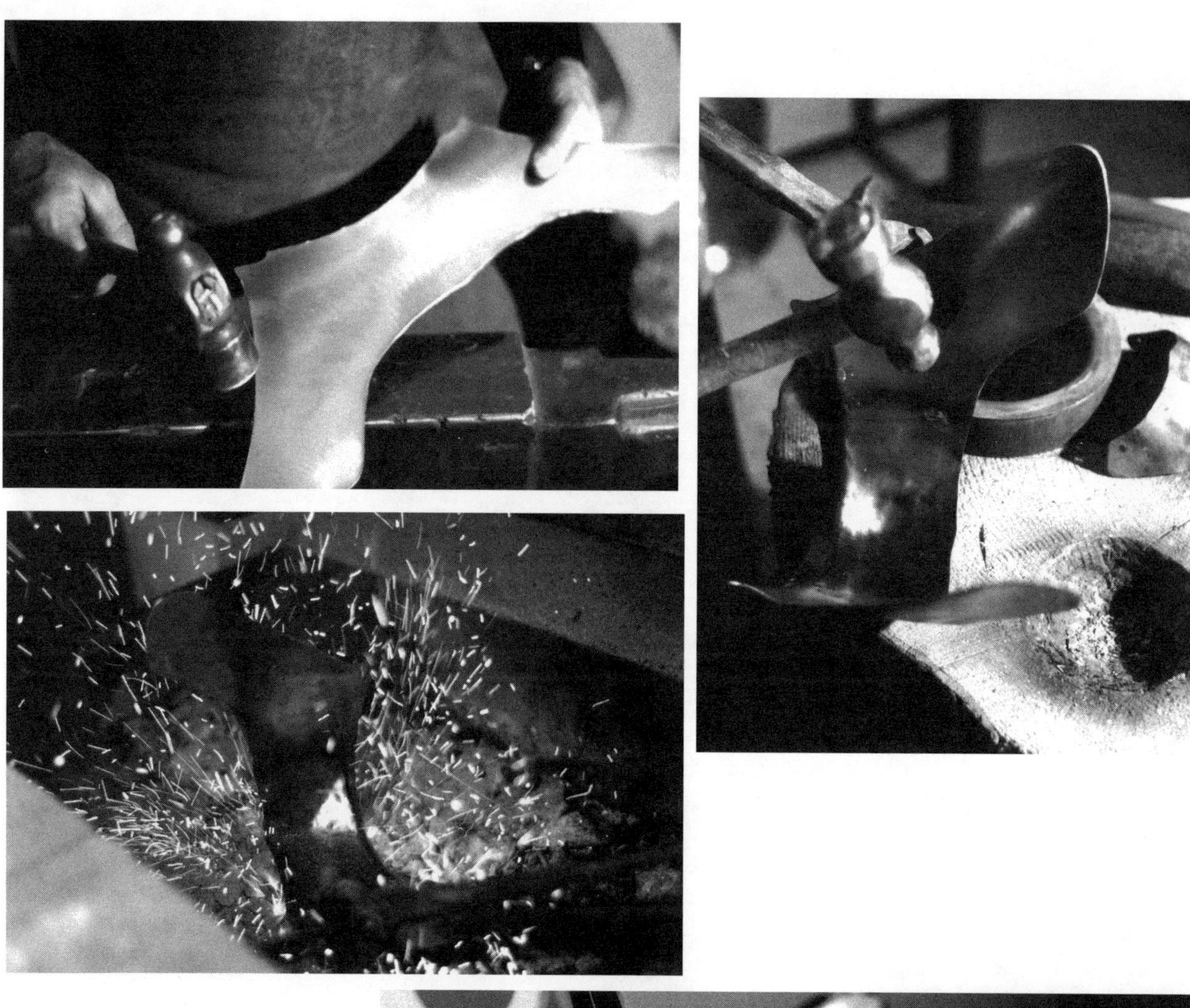

Here we are forging the bevor of a close helmet. With the amount of stretching needed for the bevor, red hot color is required.

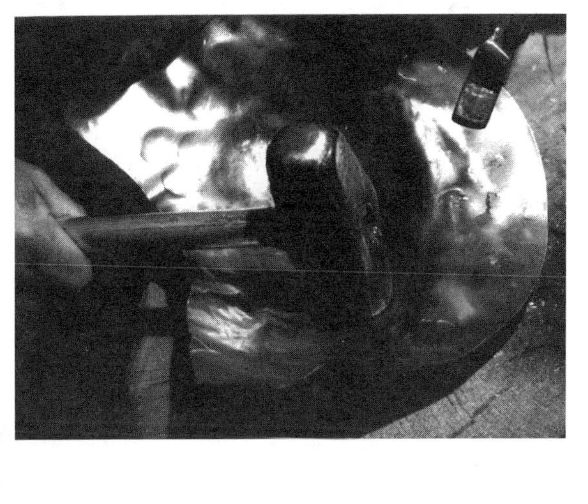

Demonstrated here is hammering half of a close helmet, and the use of a steel ring mounted on a stump. Because the heat from forging makes a wood stump deteriorate quickly, we use a steel ring for this extreme stretching.

The sabaton tip will be shown throughout its stages of development to demonstrate various processes we use.

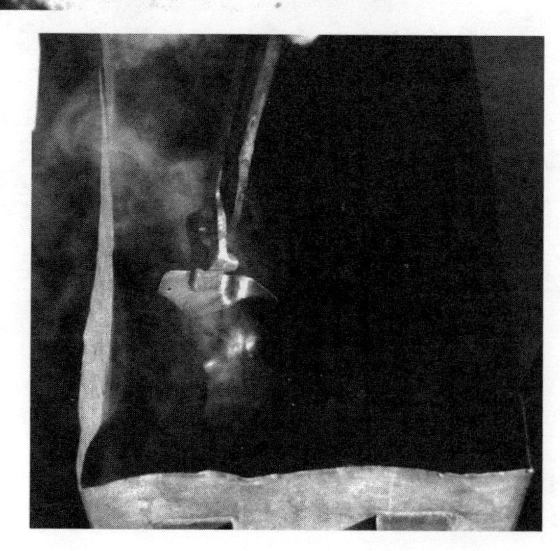

We planish, then we chisel a centre crease on the sabaton tip.

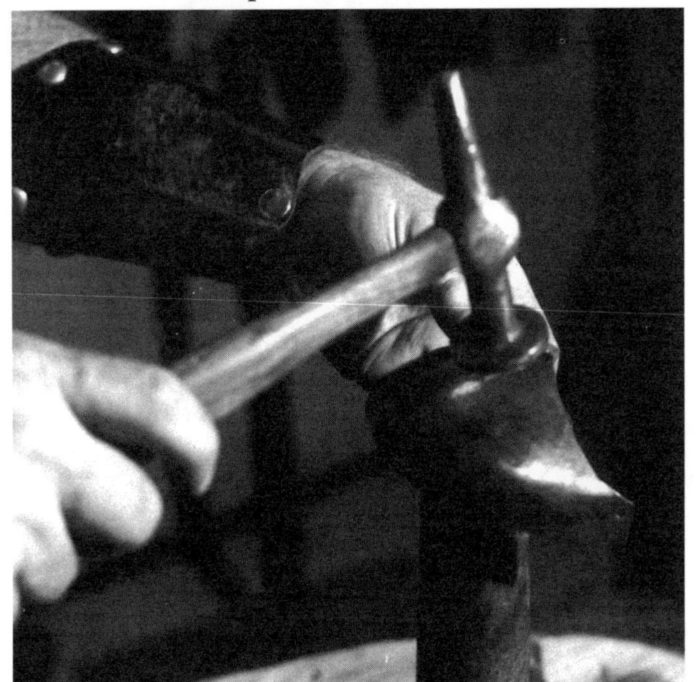

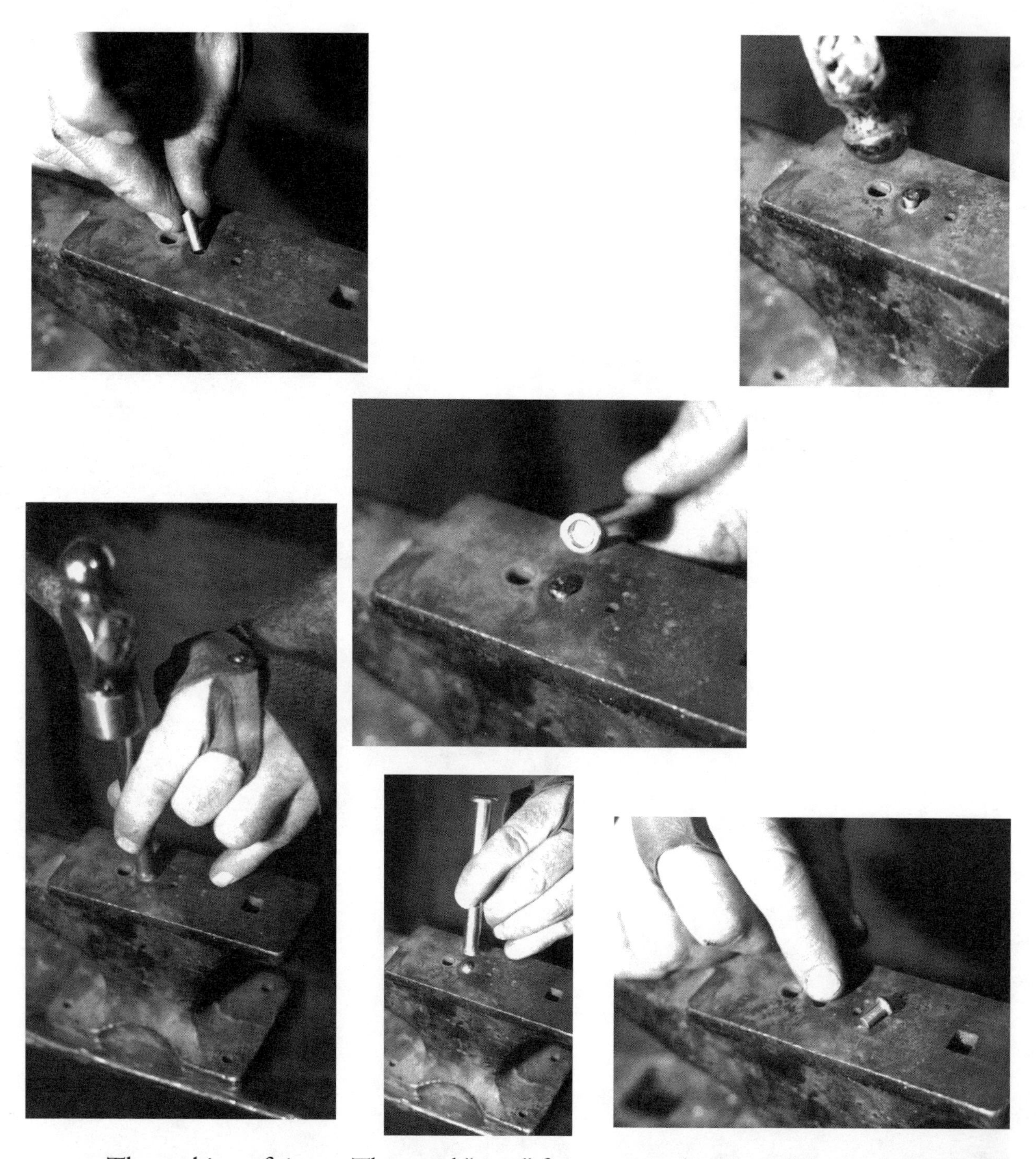

The making of rivets: The word "rivet" first appeared in chronicles in the sixteenth century. Before then, it was referred to as an arming nail, which is simply a pin or a nail with a head on one end, either flat or rounded. Rivets were often made of brass, and decorated, depending on their function.

We've made a special anvil for just this. First, a steel pin is put in a steel slot, then the end is hammered to make a head. This can be done hot or cold, but it is easier hot. Then a special chisel (with a round head grooved out in the end) is used to hammer on the pin's top to make a uniform size rivet.

Because historically there weren't any drills, and there may have been inconsistencies in hole sizes, we've tried different ways of recreating accurate holes. The best, and simplest way is to punch a hole with a pointed chisel, and file it to it's appropriate size. Here we demonstrate this technique on a sabaton lame.

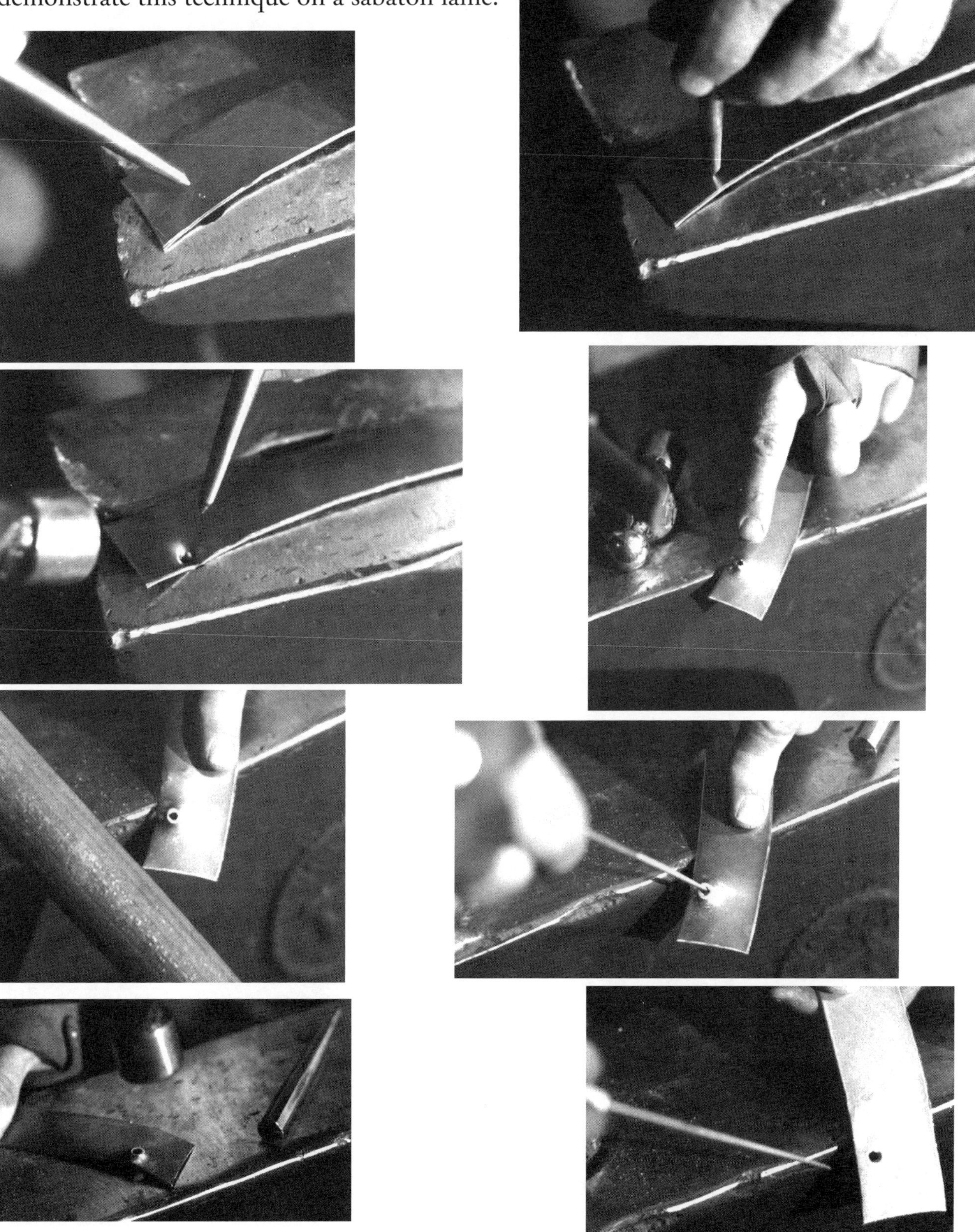

We now rivet the sabaton pieces together.

All buckles were handmade by the armourer, although eventually there were businesses that would supply them with buckles. These were either cast or hand-forged. Above and on the three following pages, we demonstrate how a simple single loop buckle is made.

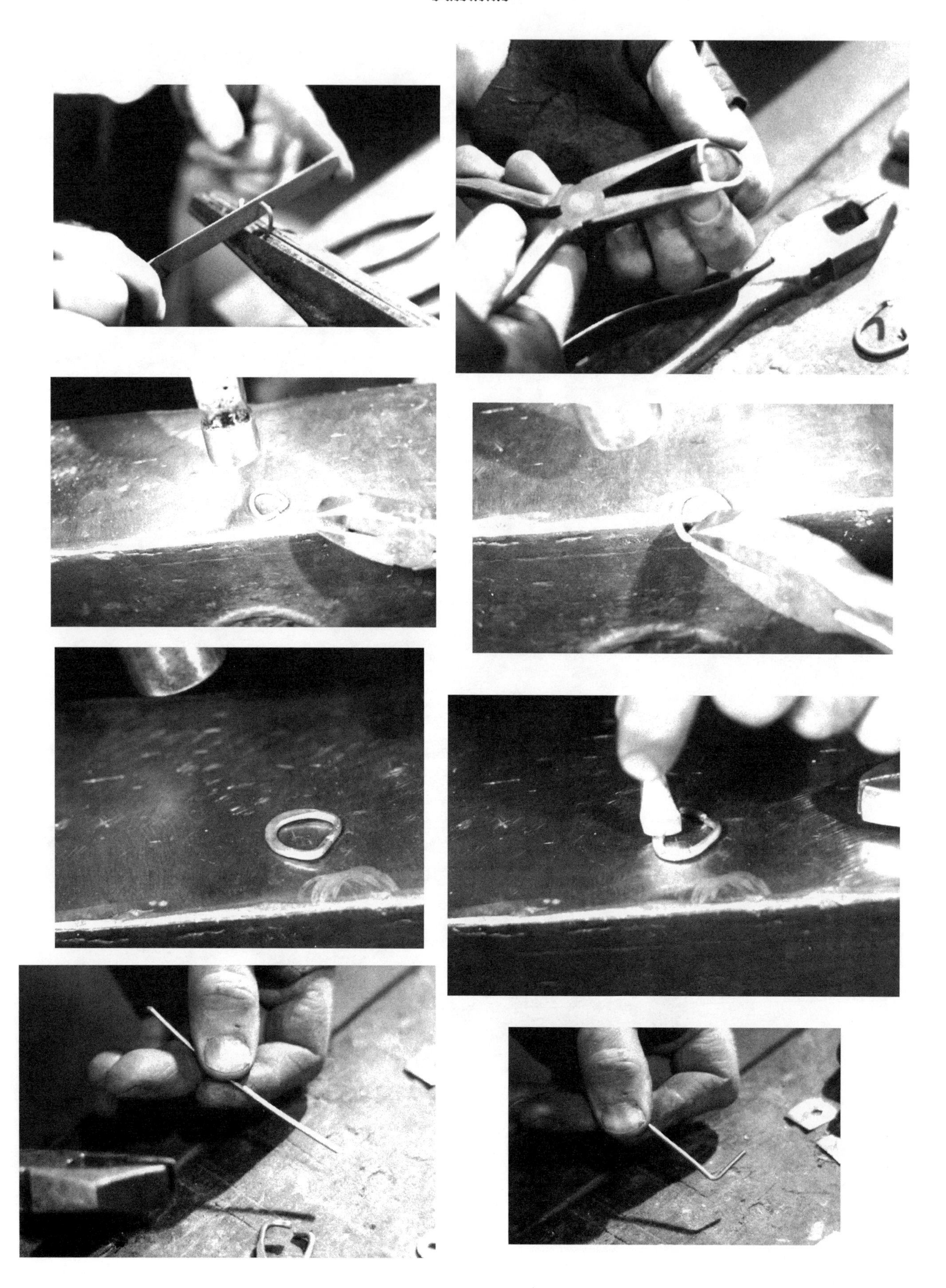

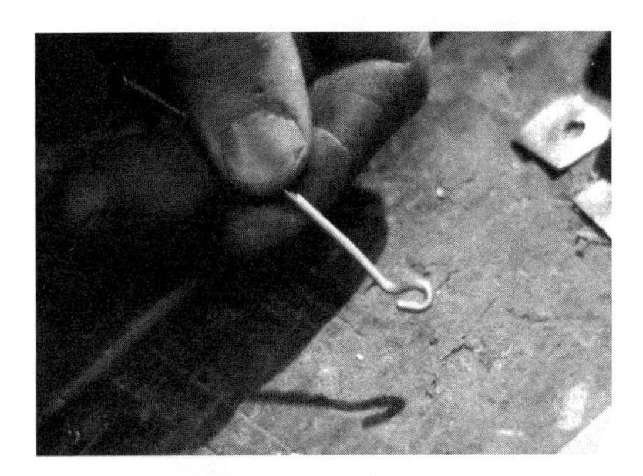

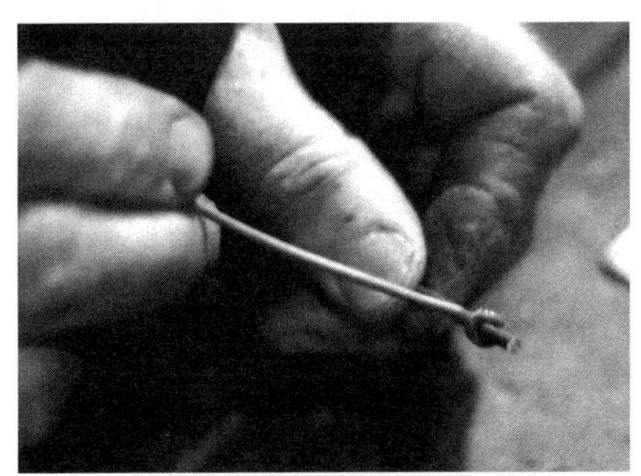

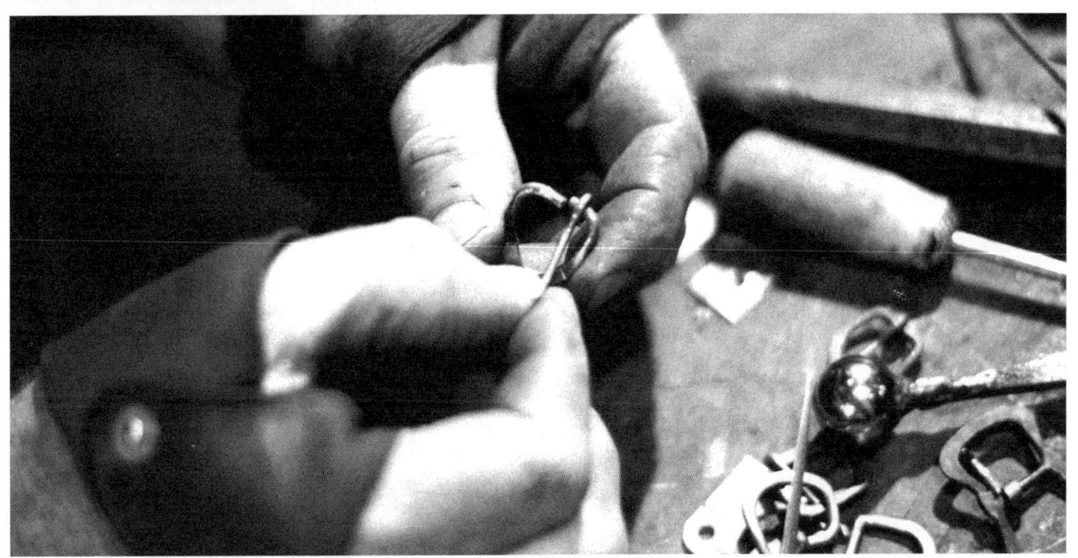

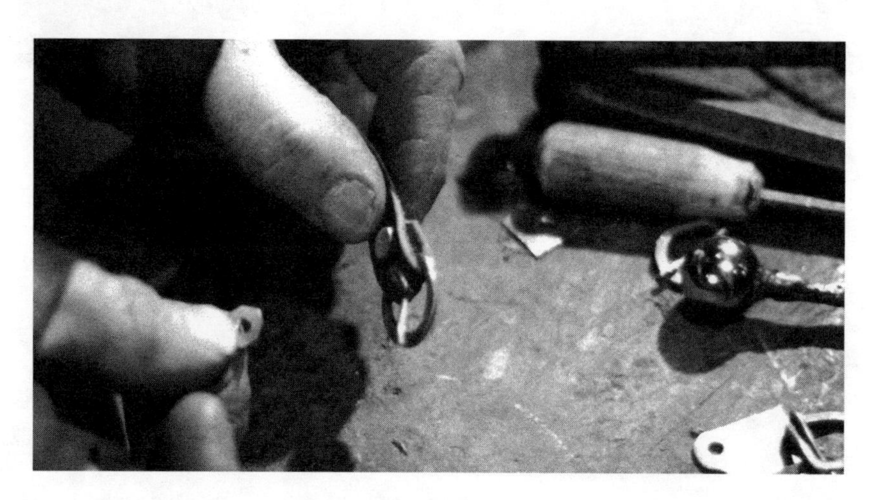

We hand-make hinges to fit the style and function of each suit, usually decorated with chiseled designs. This is a basic style hinge. The pin would normally be forged hot. This one is formed cold.

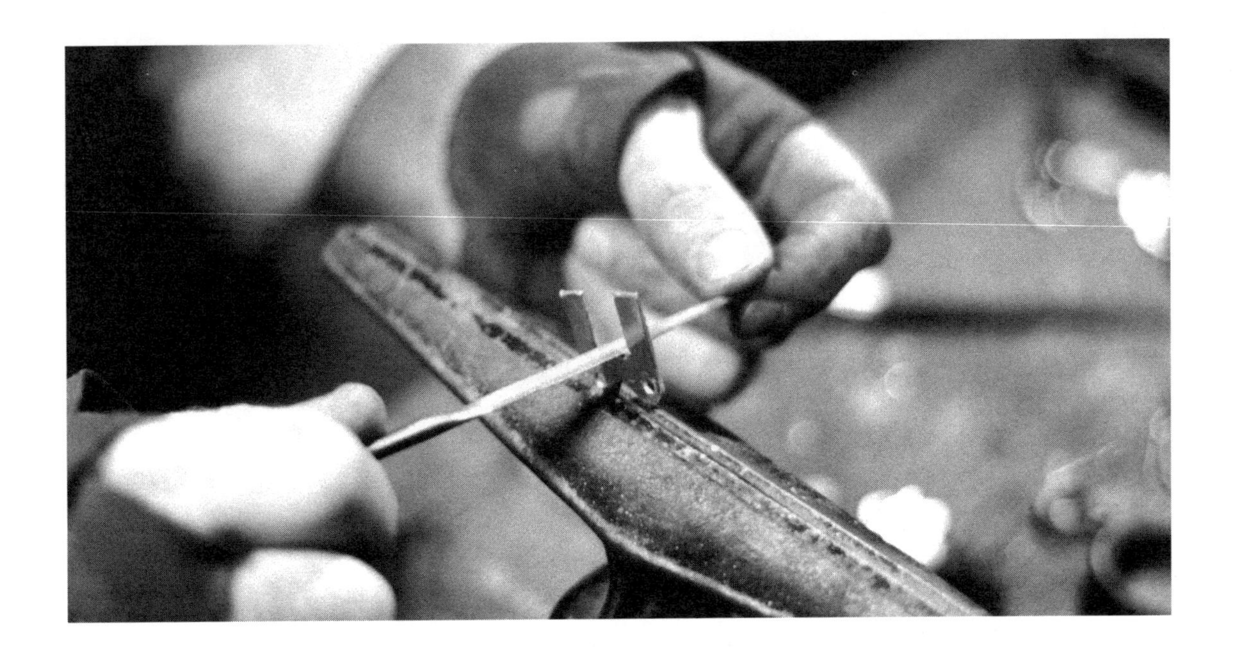

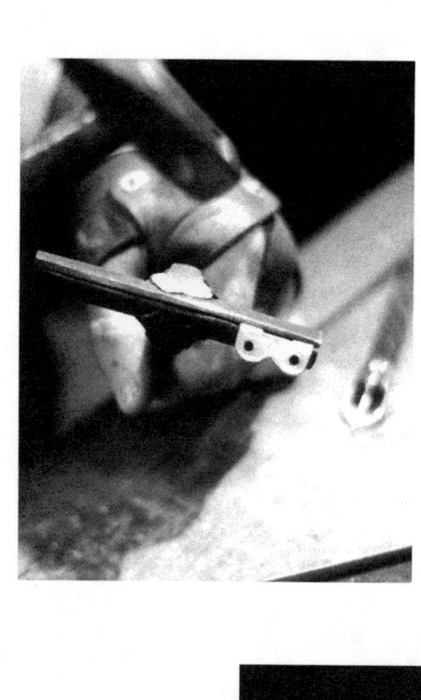

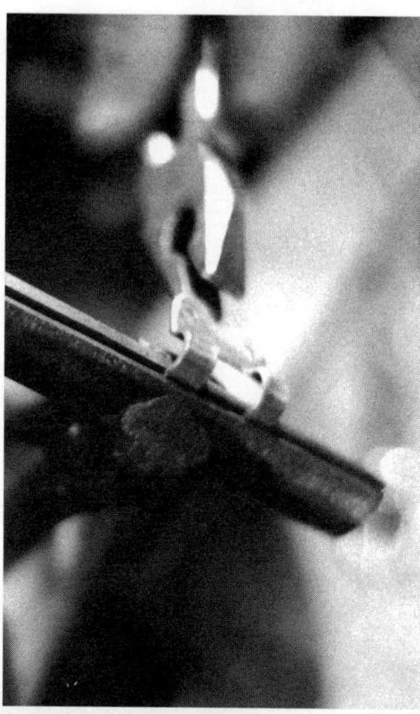

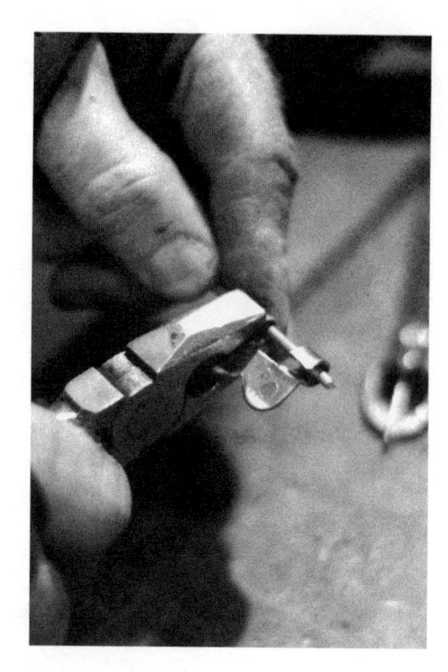

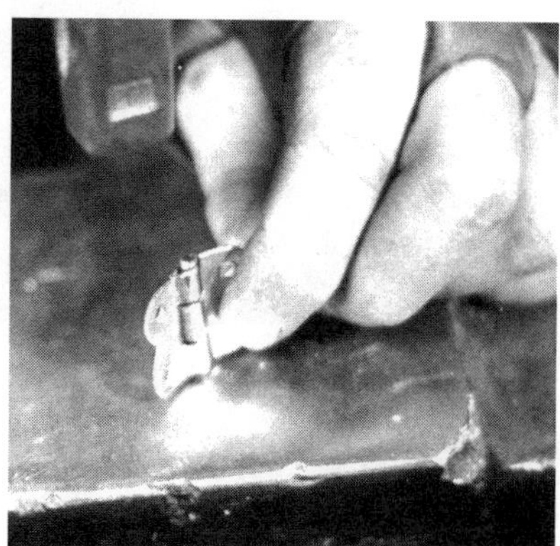

The Greaves: After planishing and filing the greave pieces, they are riveted together.

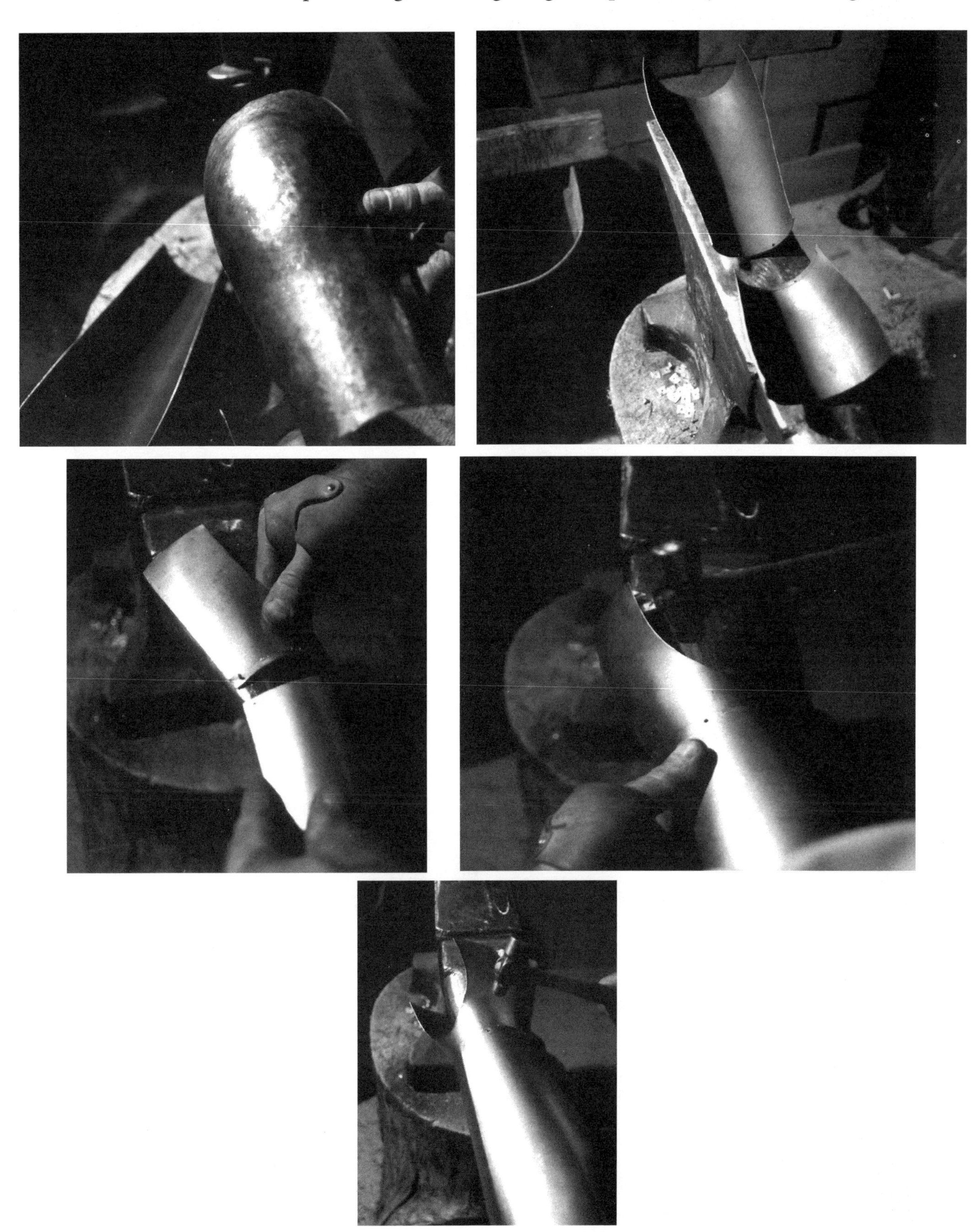

This is how hinges are riveted to the two greave halves. Historically, greaves were held together by a buckle and strap, but the use of buckles and straps gave way to hooks and pins, probably due to straps being cut or worn off.

We use pins to hinge the greaves together.

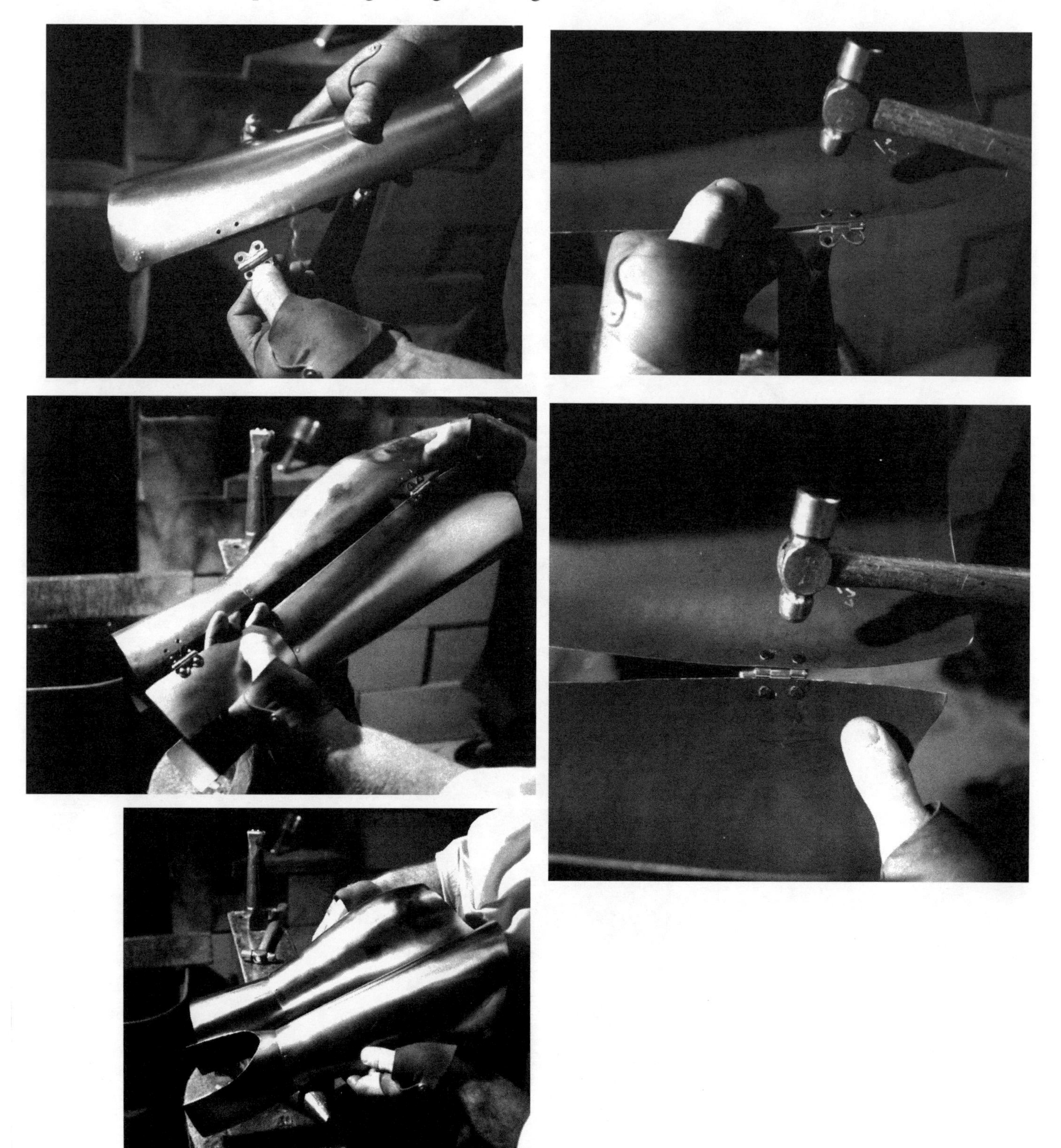

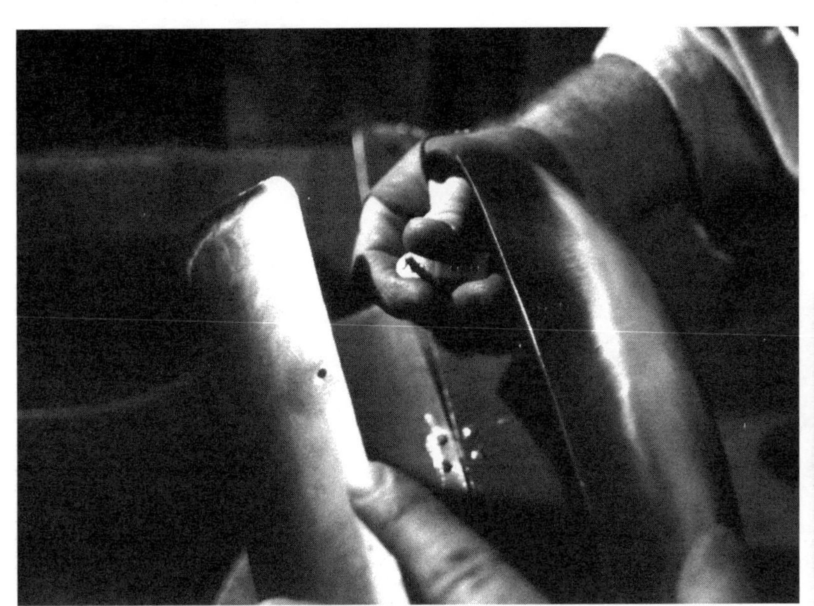

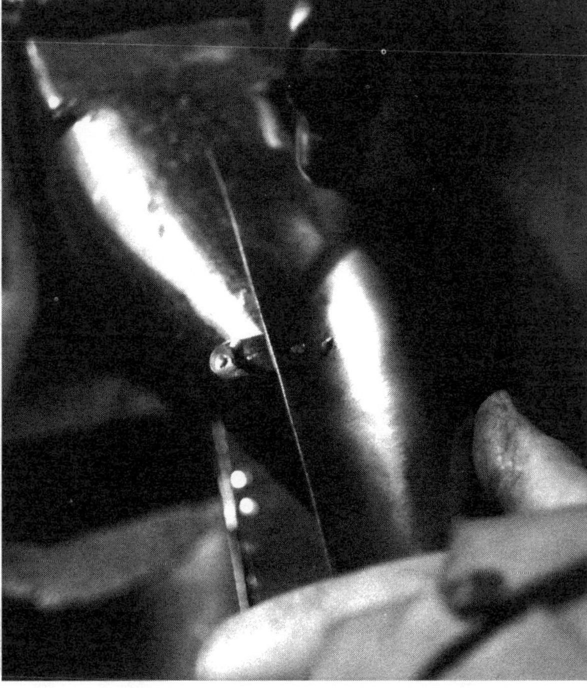

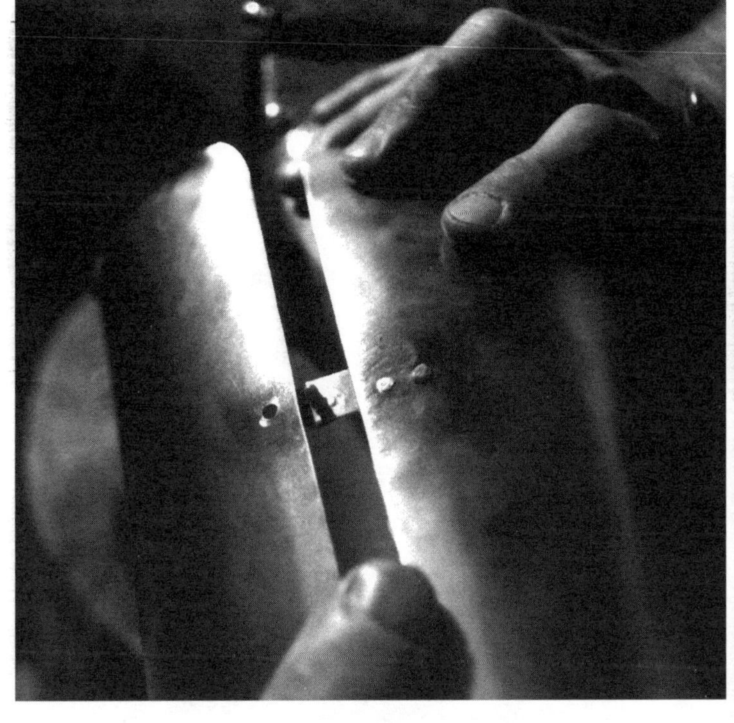

Sabatons were originally separate pieces of armour, but experiments with function eventually made it possible to attach them to the greaves. Some models have pins to make the sabatons removable. We're showing the sabaton attached with rivets.

The knee cop is heated to stretch it. It is then planished, and a centre ridge is chiseled out.

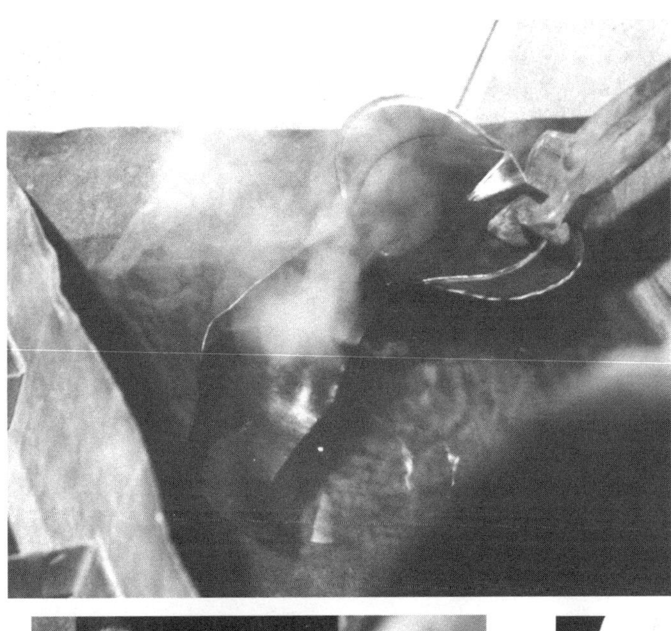

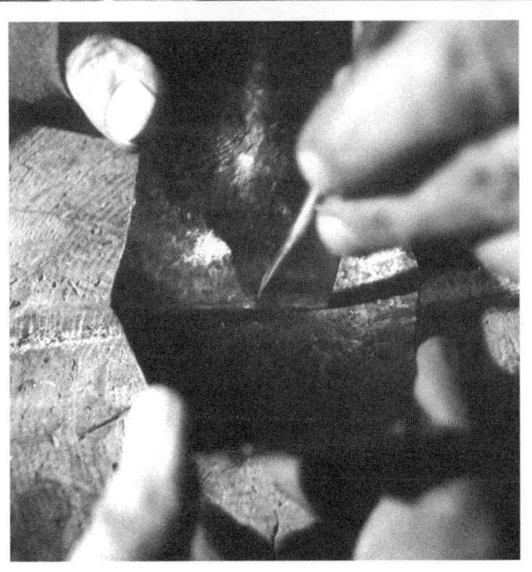

A crease is put in the centre ridge in the knee laminations, then riveted to the knee cop.

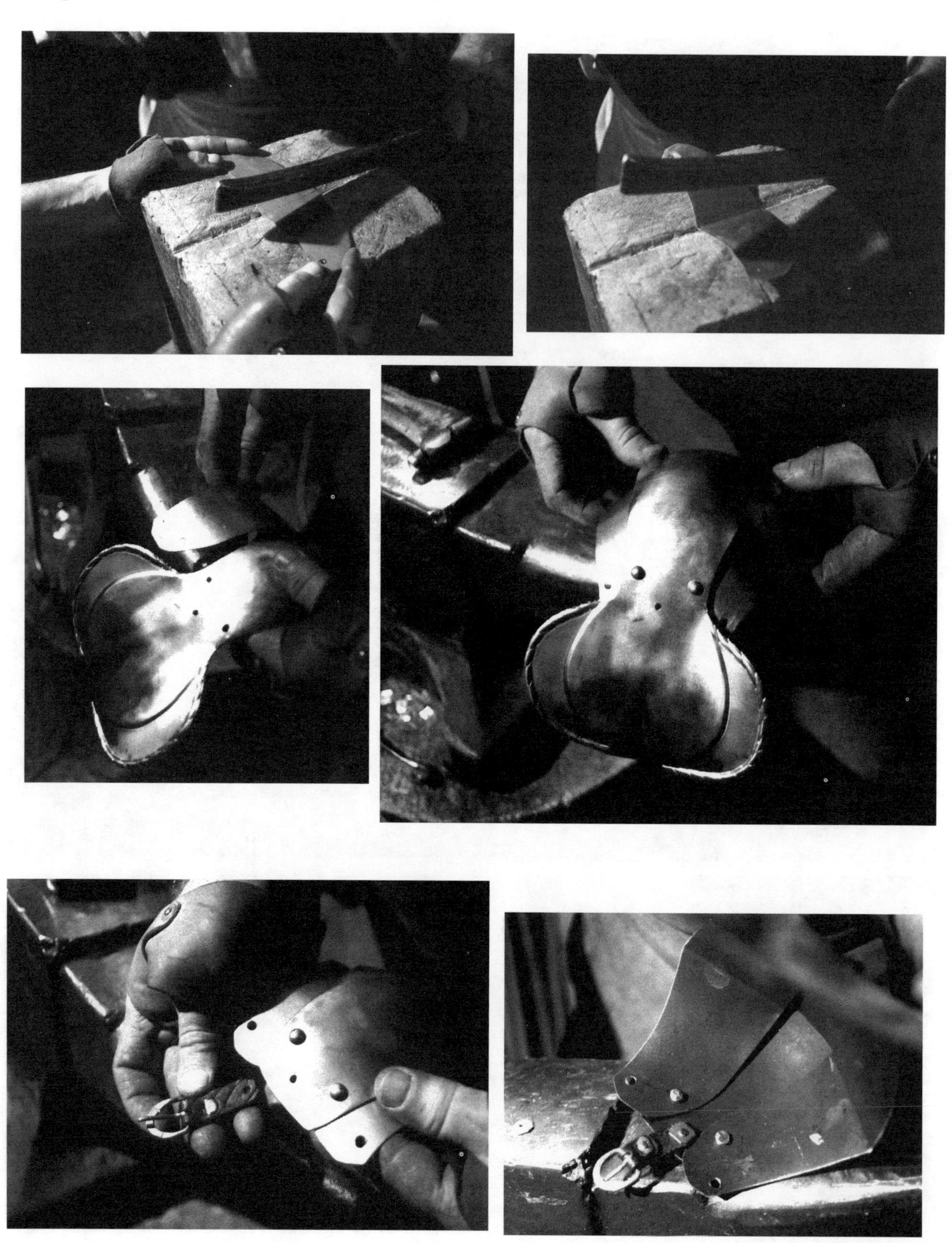

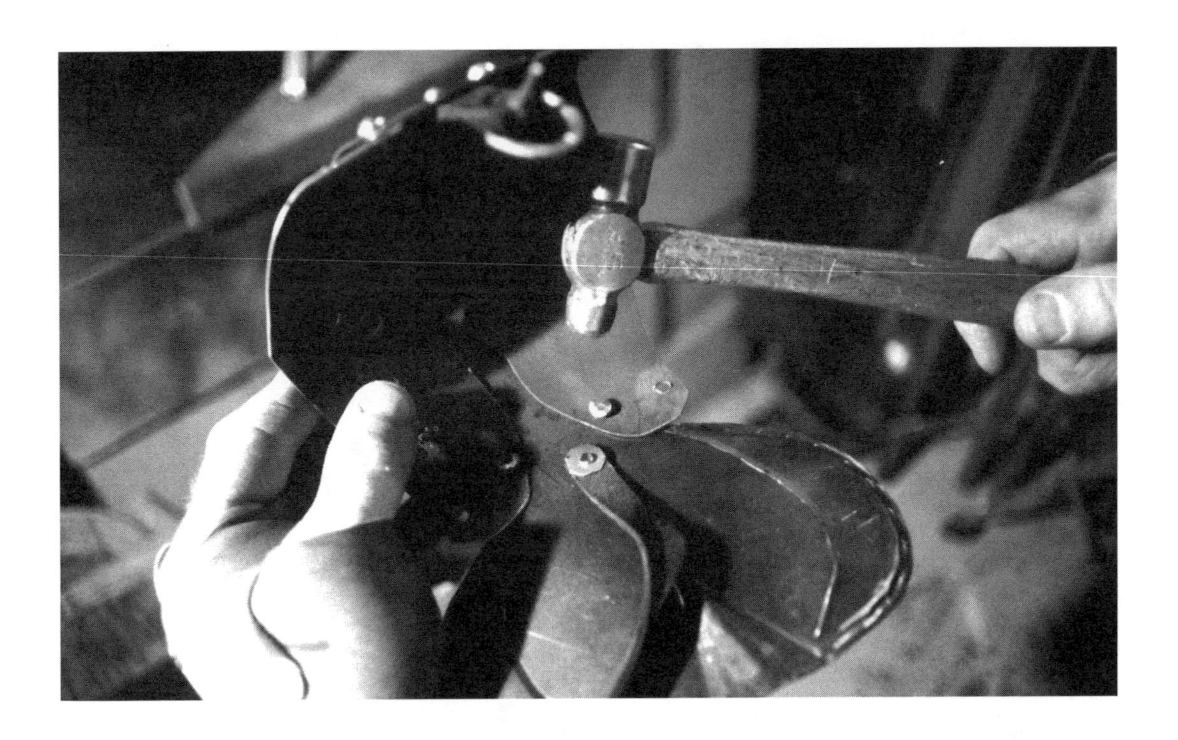

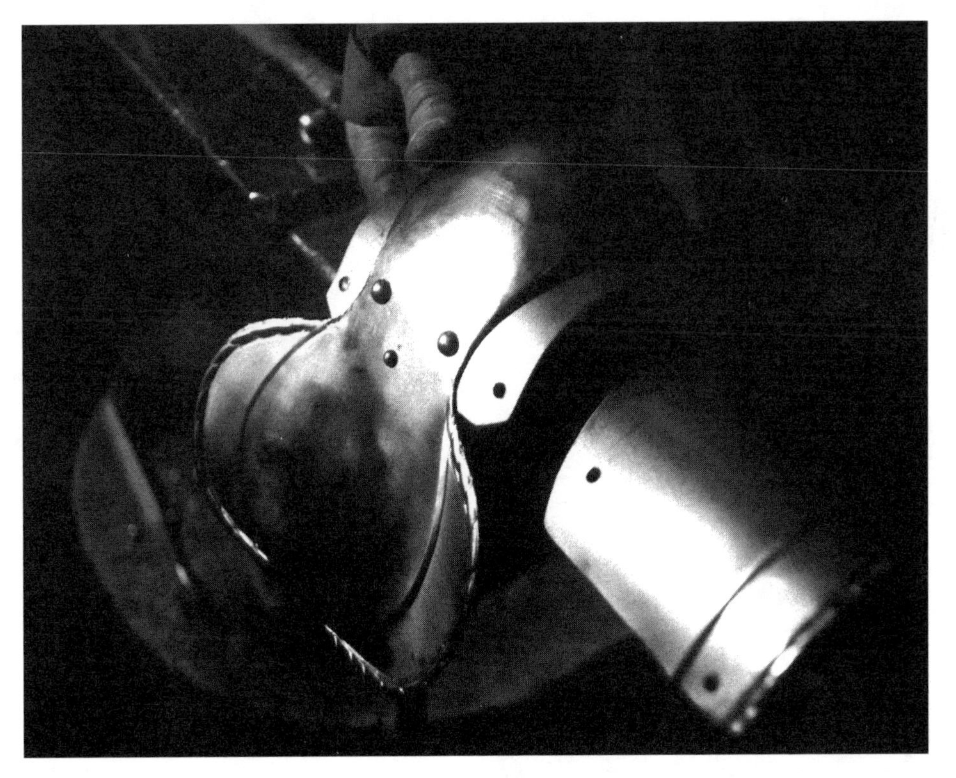

We rivet the strap and top of the greave lamination.

To prepare the cuisse, first the edge is rolled to give it more strength. Then a rope design is chiseled in, which was fashionable for the time.

We chisel a drop ledge, and punch out holes for the leather liner.

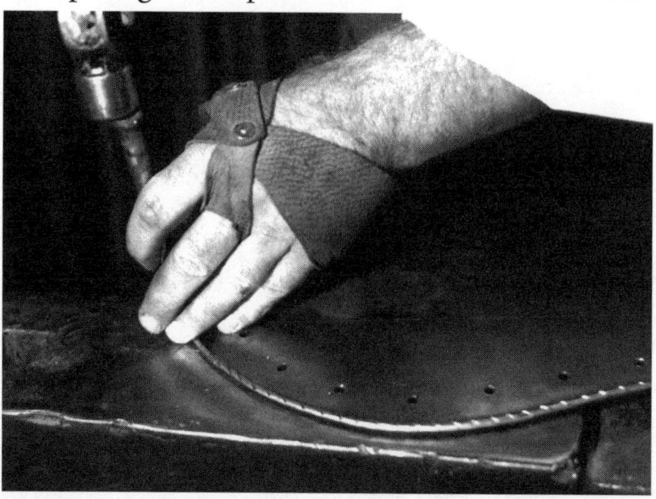

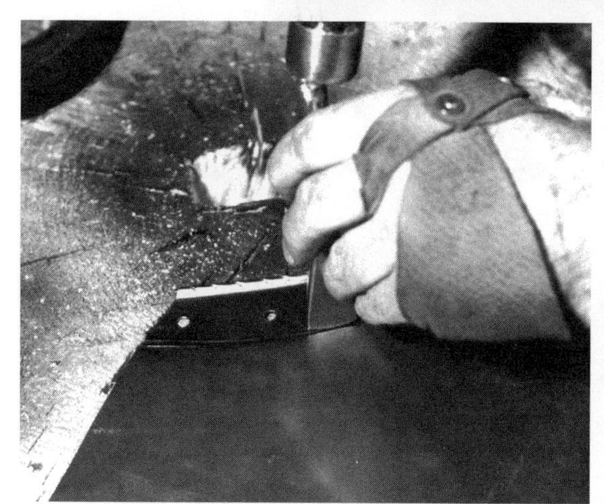

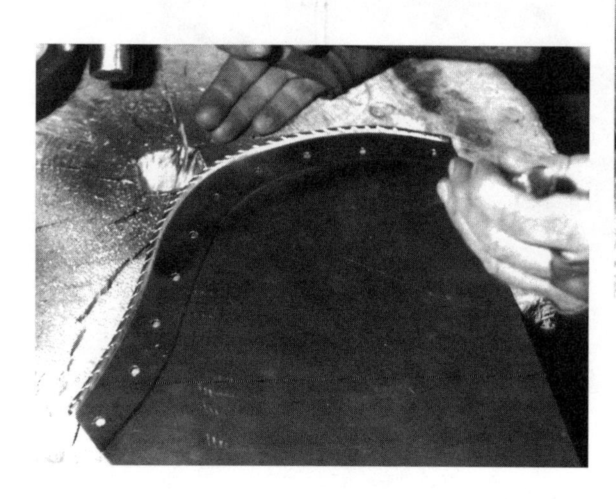

Here, we demonstrate how to make medieval washers, which historically had several uses. They were probably made and kept in stock by the armourer's apprentices.

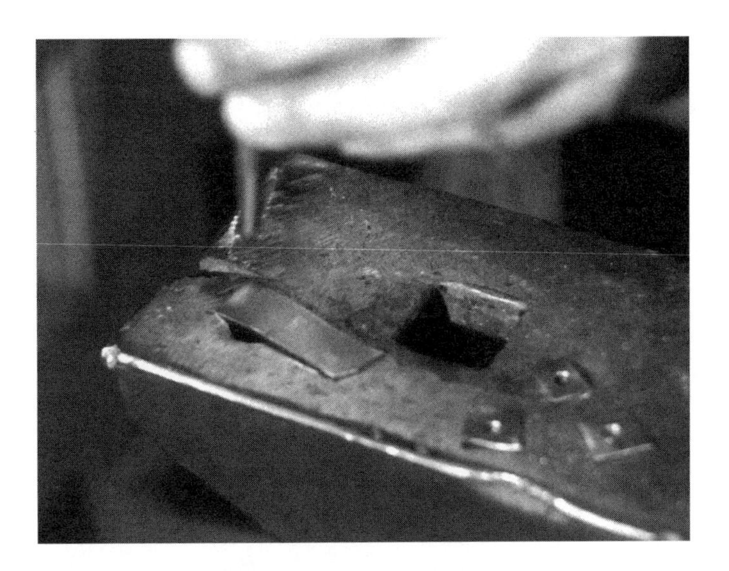

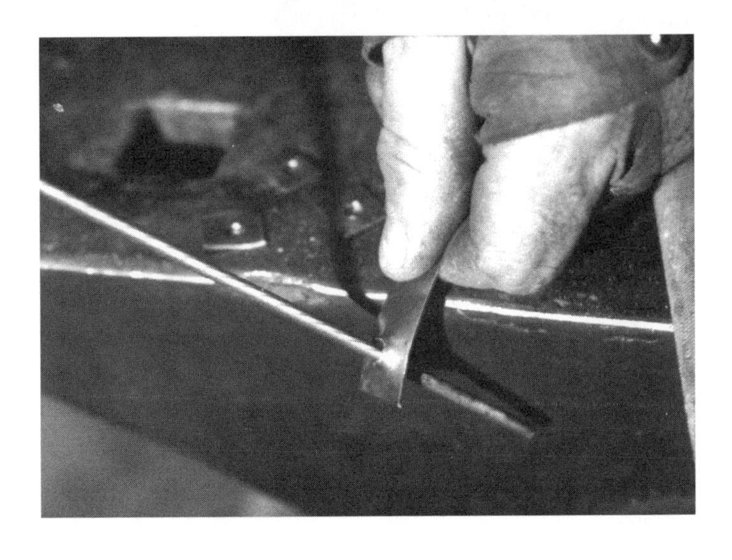

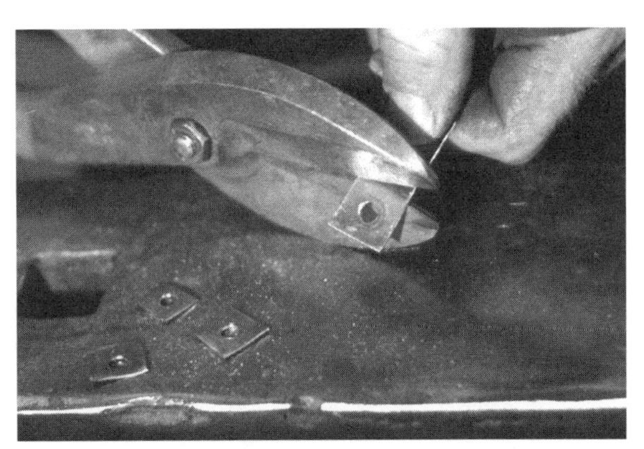

The armourer would have employed other craftsmen related to the industry. Leather workers would have created strapping, lining, and gloves. A leather liner is made for the cuisse.

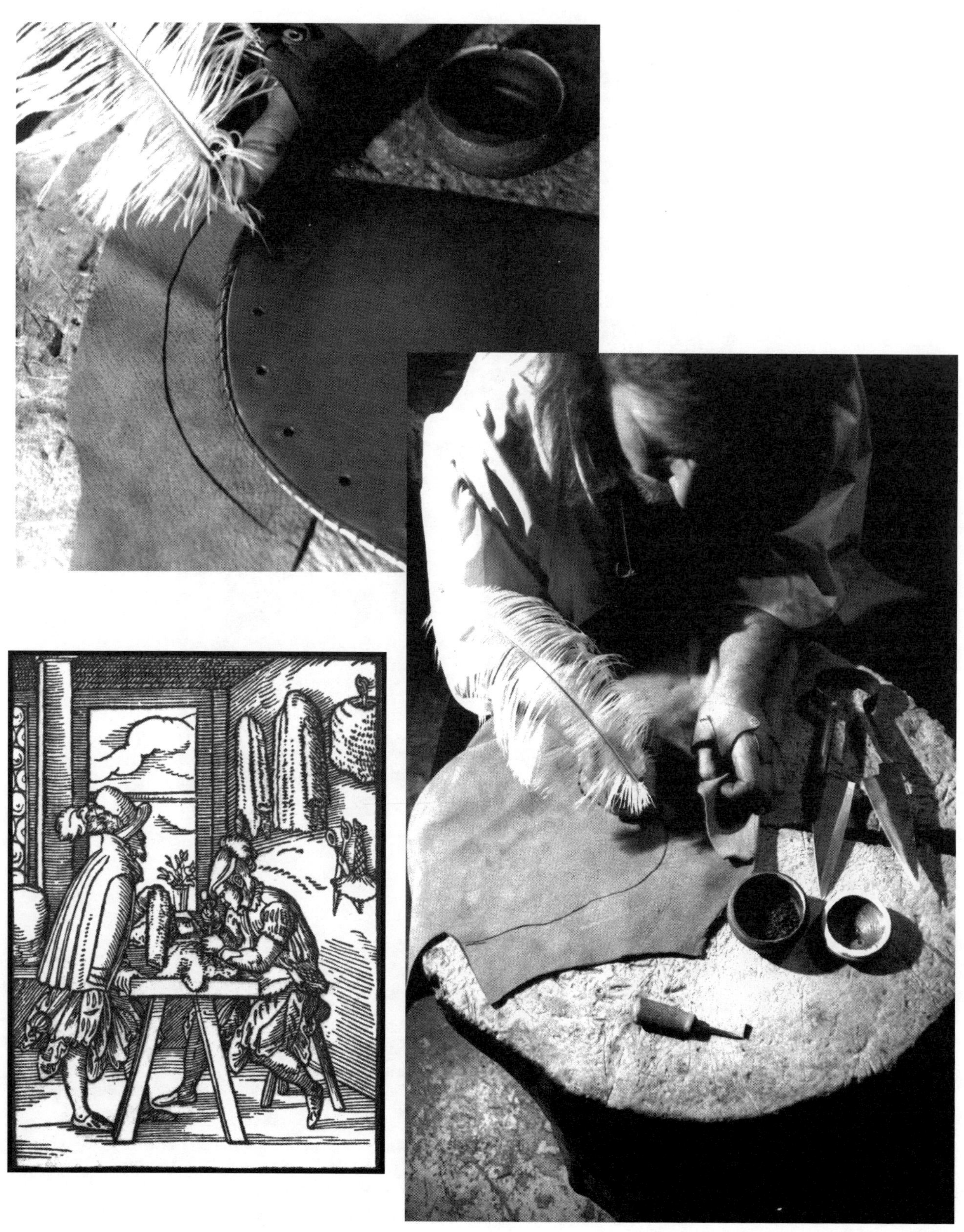

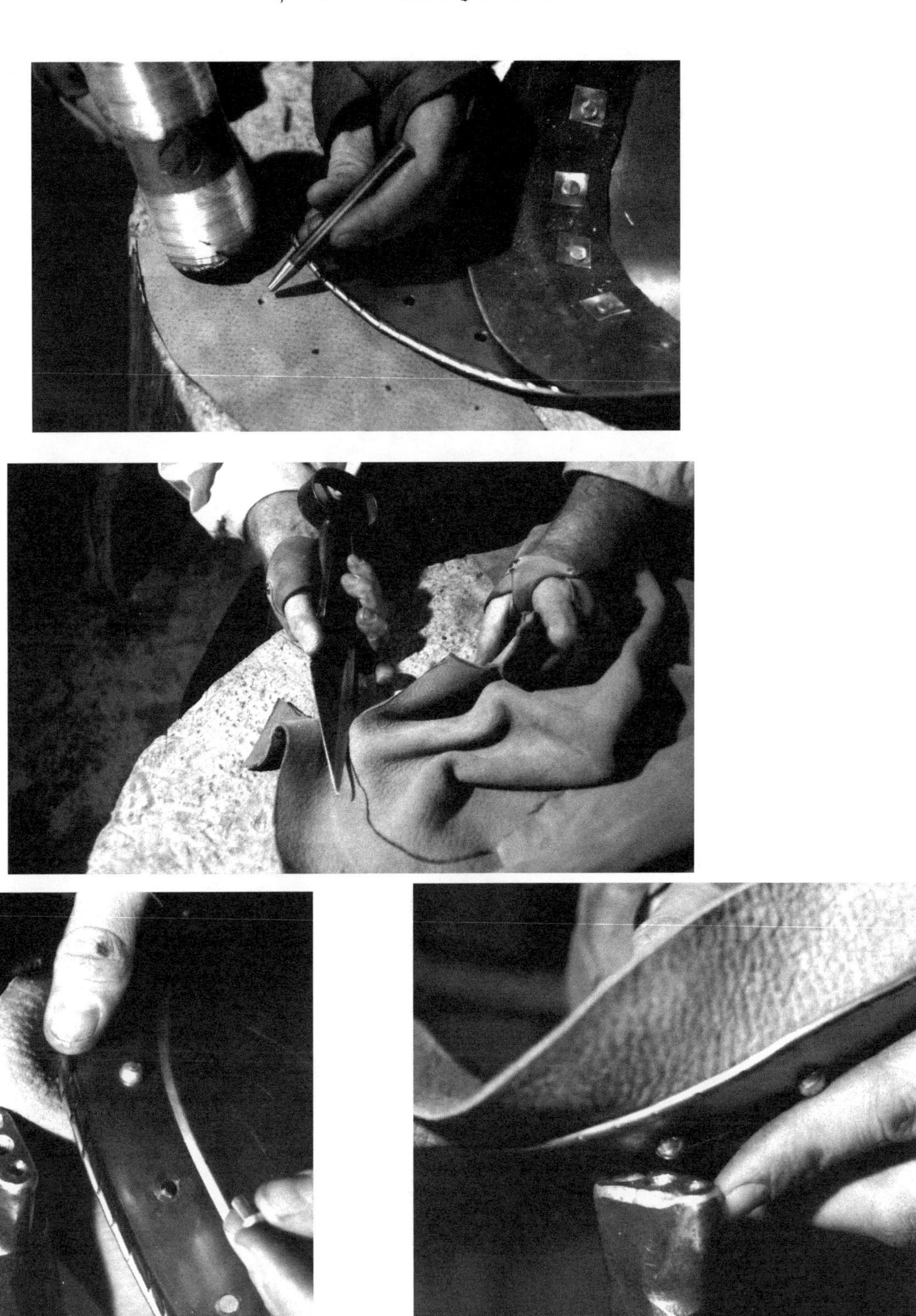

Take notice of the two tools in this picture: One is a hole punch for the leather holes, and the other is a rivet set. This set is necessary so the rivet head will maintain it's shape while being riveted to something.

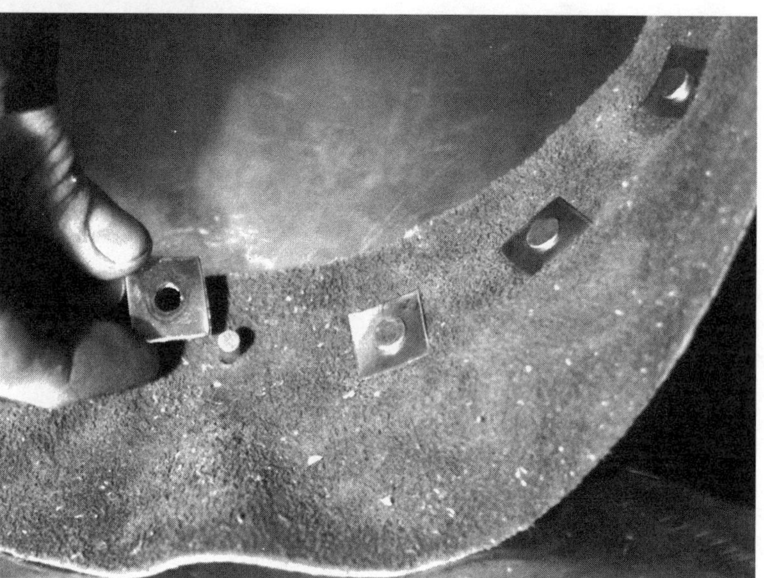

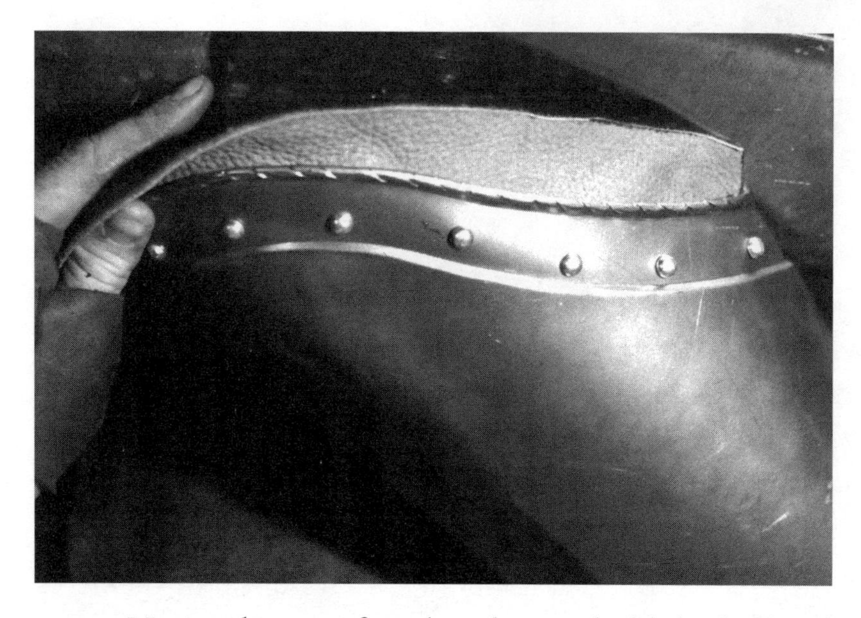

Notice the use of steel washers to hold the leather lining for the leg.

The cuisse is now attached to the knee cop, and the articulation is checked for any adjustments needed.

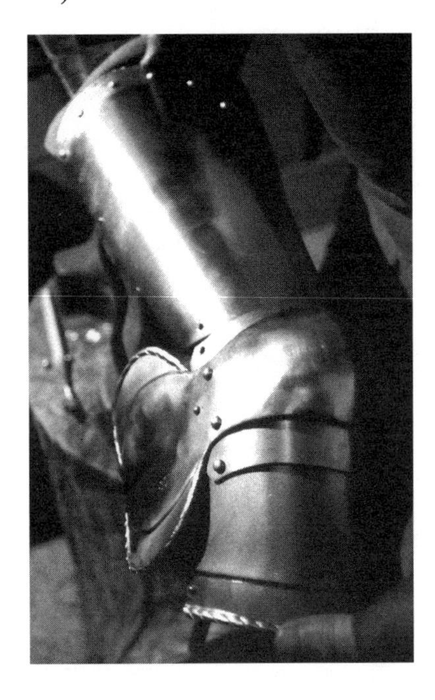

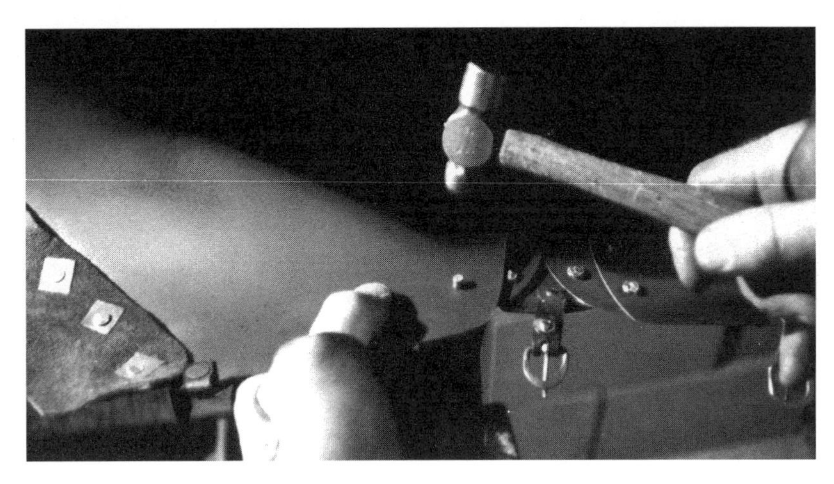

Rolling machines (called burring machines) have been documented in the seventeenth century, but we surmise they were probably pioneered in the sixteenth century, because the Maximilian style suits of the time had extensive ribbing on them. We use this modern machine to demonstrate its use.

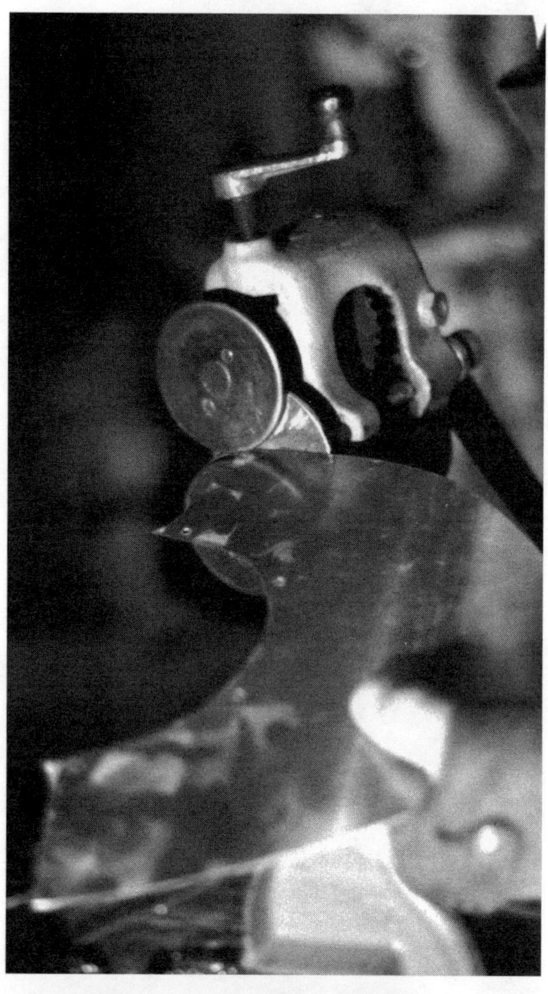

These photos show how wire was put inside the roll to further strengthen the edges of armour parts.

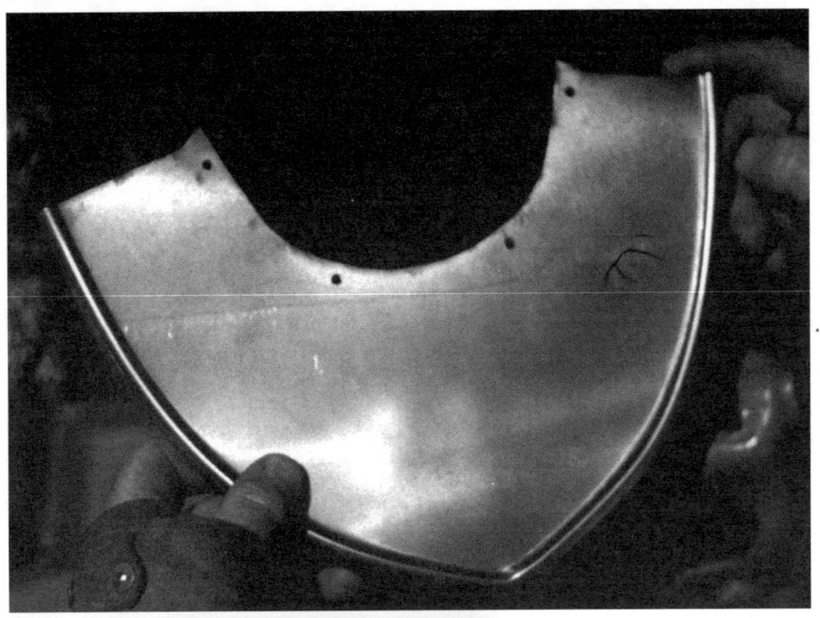

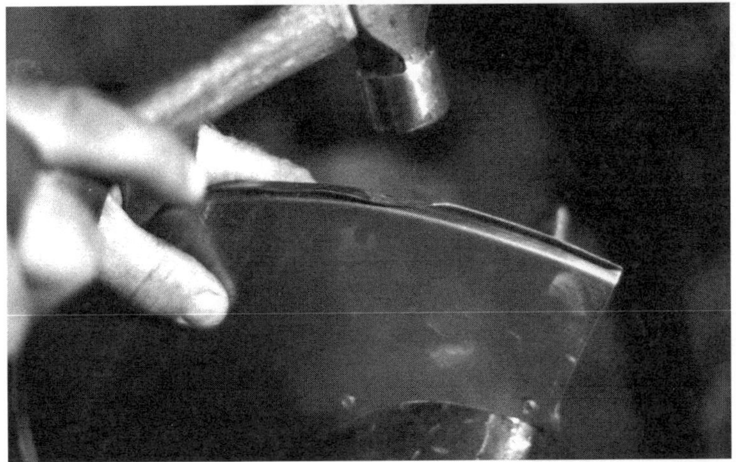

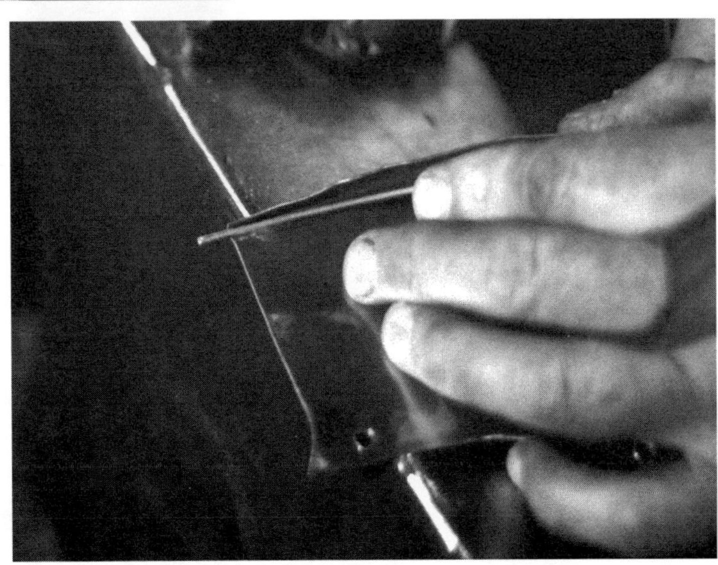

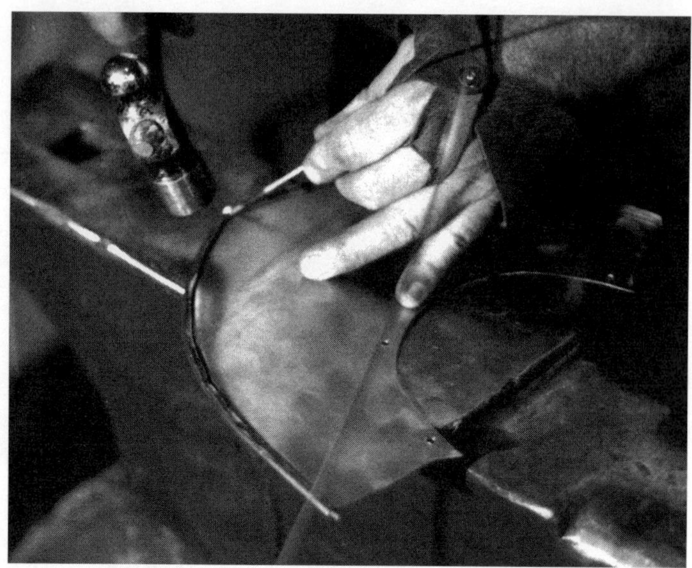

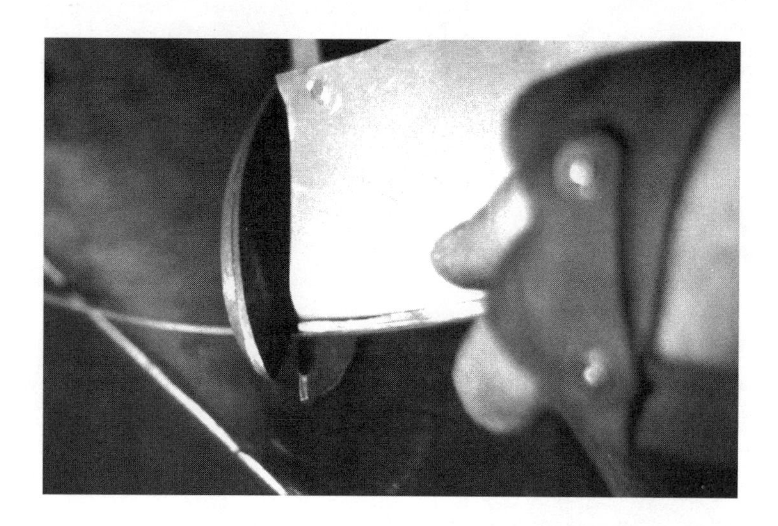

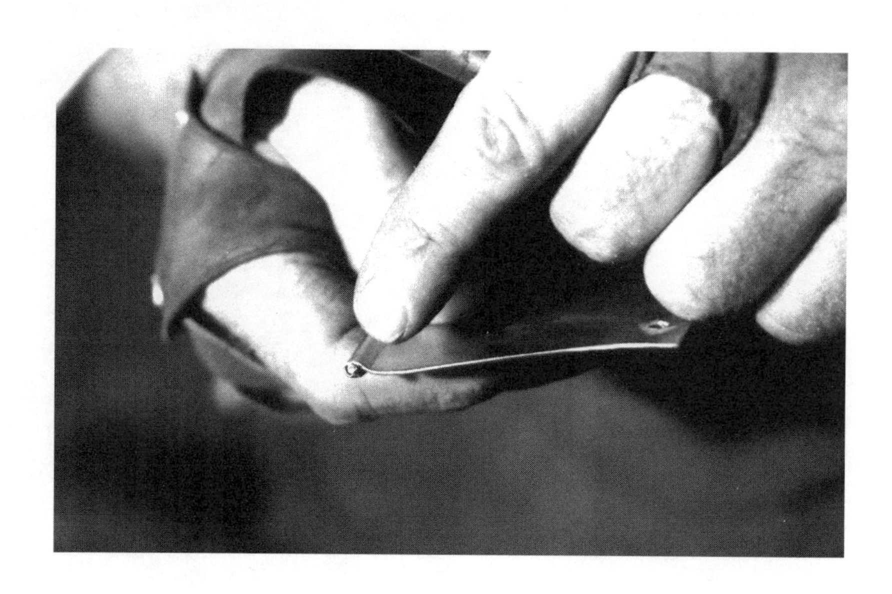

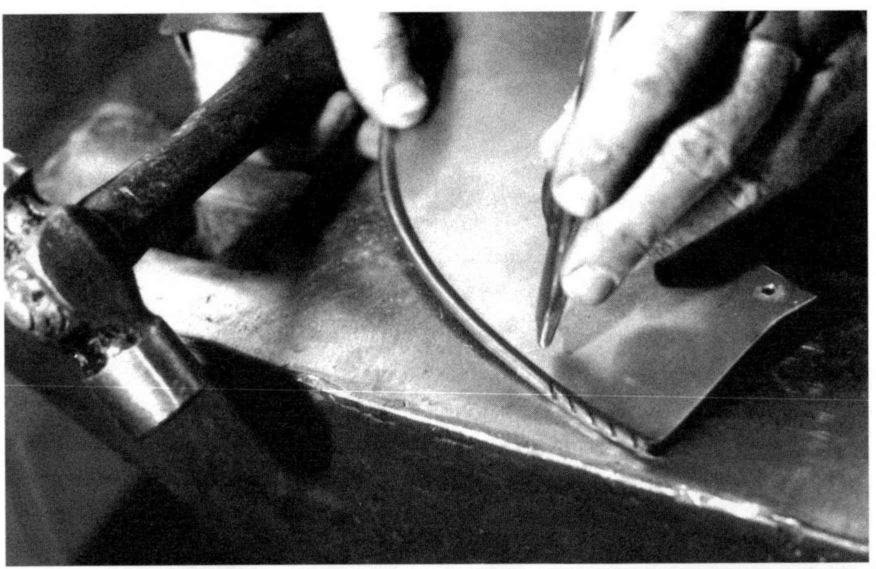

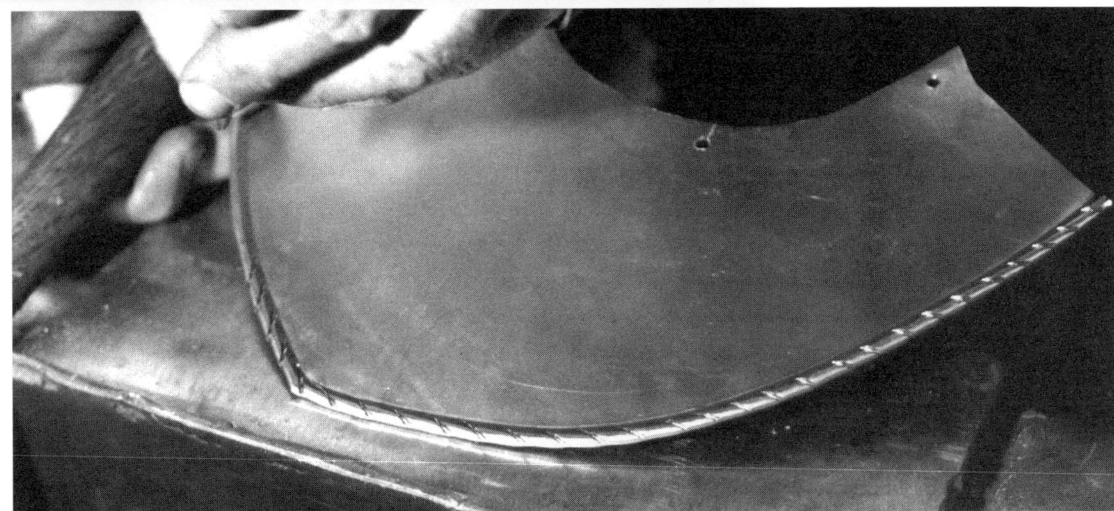

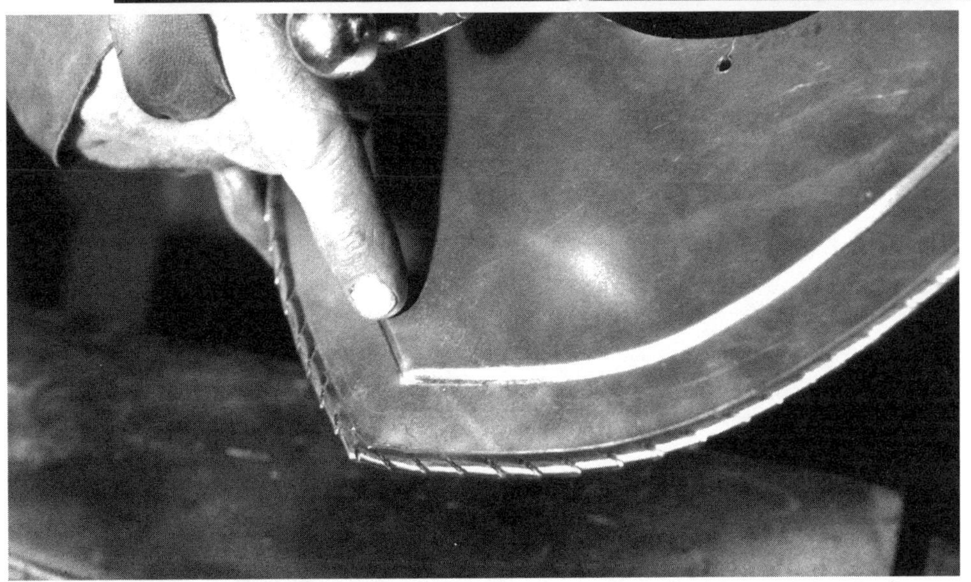

We've chiseled a rope design on the edge. Then a drop ledge is chiseled out on the inner side.

The gorget shaping is finished, then the pieces are riveted together. The shoulder straps and buckle with strap are then attached.

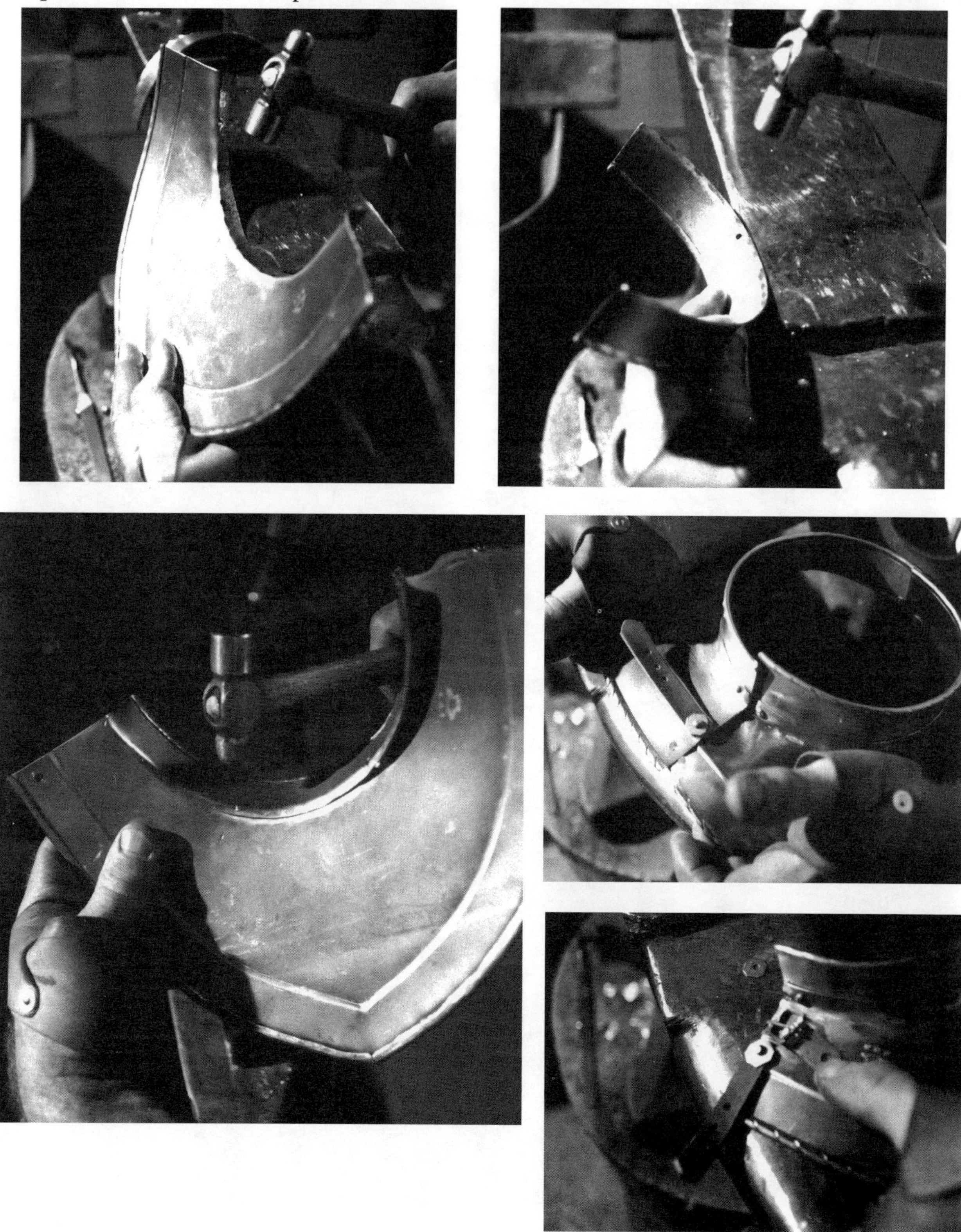

The breastplate and backplate are forged on wood stumps and anvils.

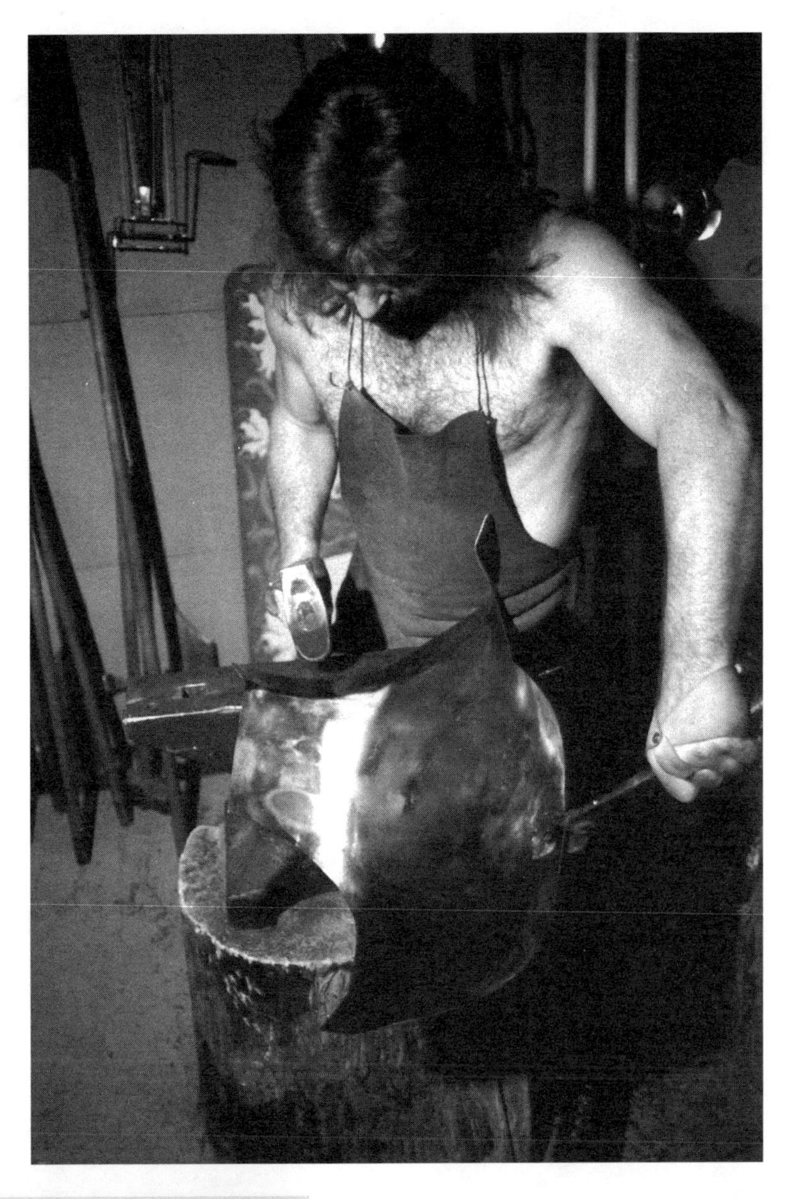

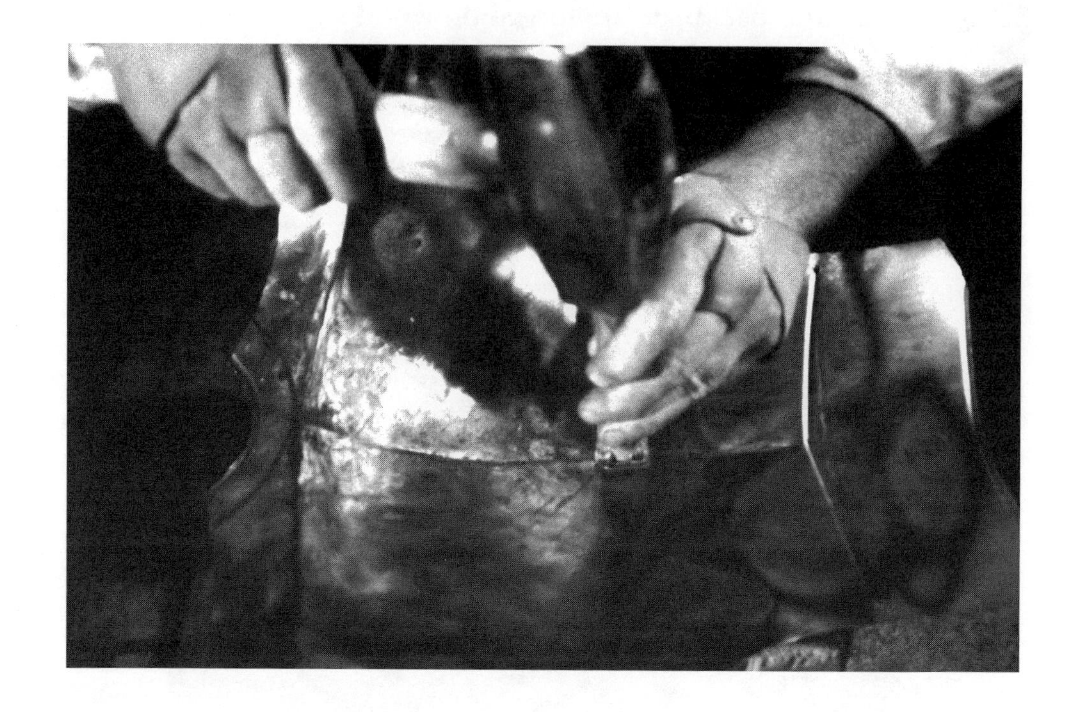

The centre ridge is punched out, then planished, picked, and filed until it's complete.

After finishing the breastplate, the slotted gussets are attached with rivets and washers.

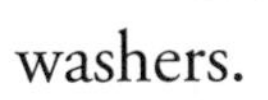

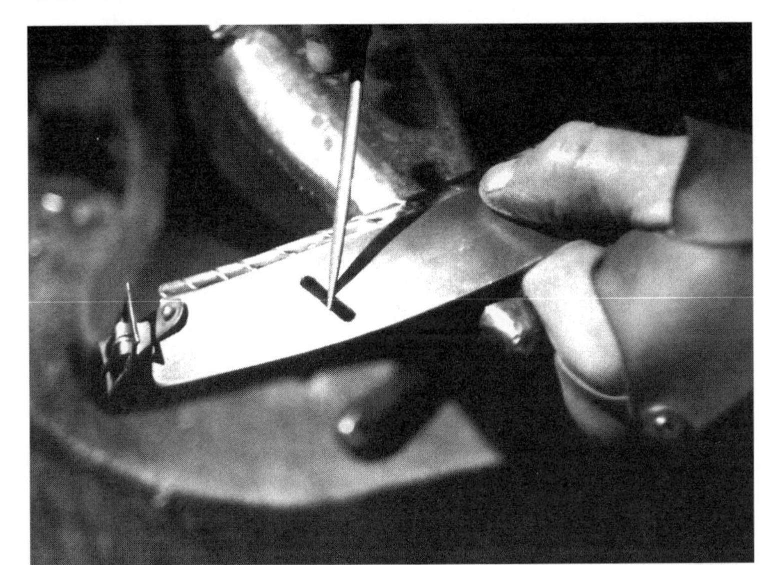

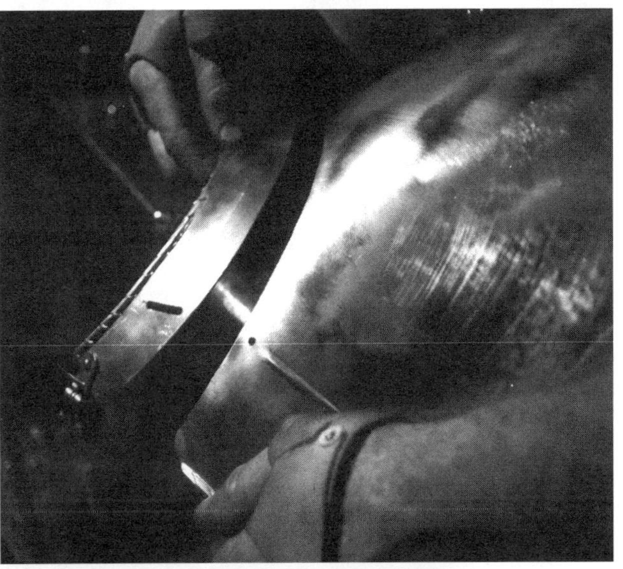

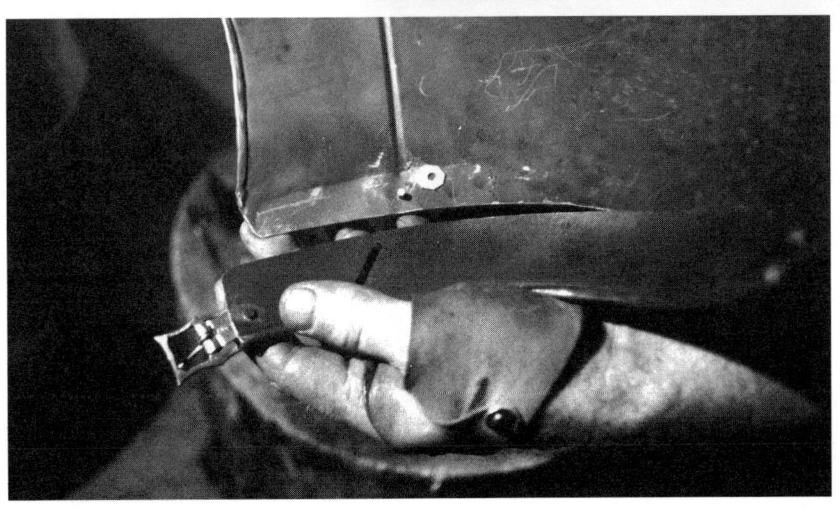

The customer for this suit wants an optional lance rest, which can be removed for field battles. Nuts and bolts were being used in the sixteenth century, including wing nuts. These may have been invented by armourers for easily removing visors and other pieces.

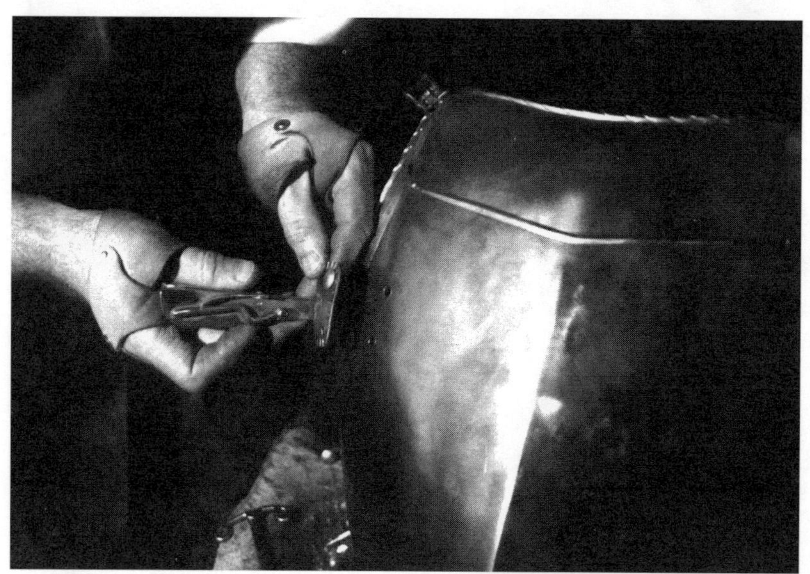

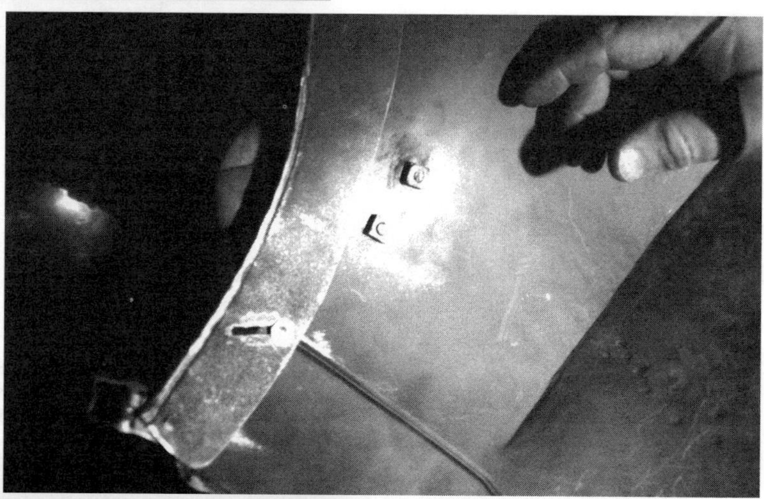

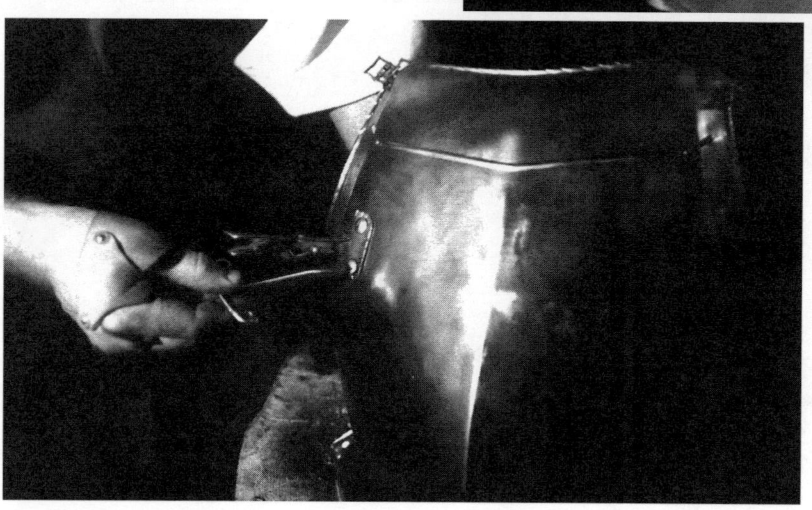

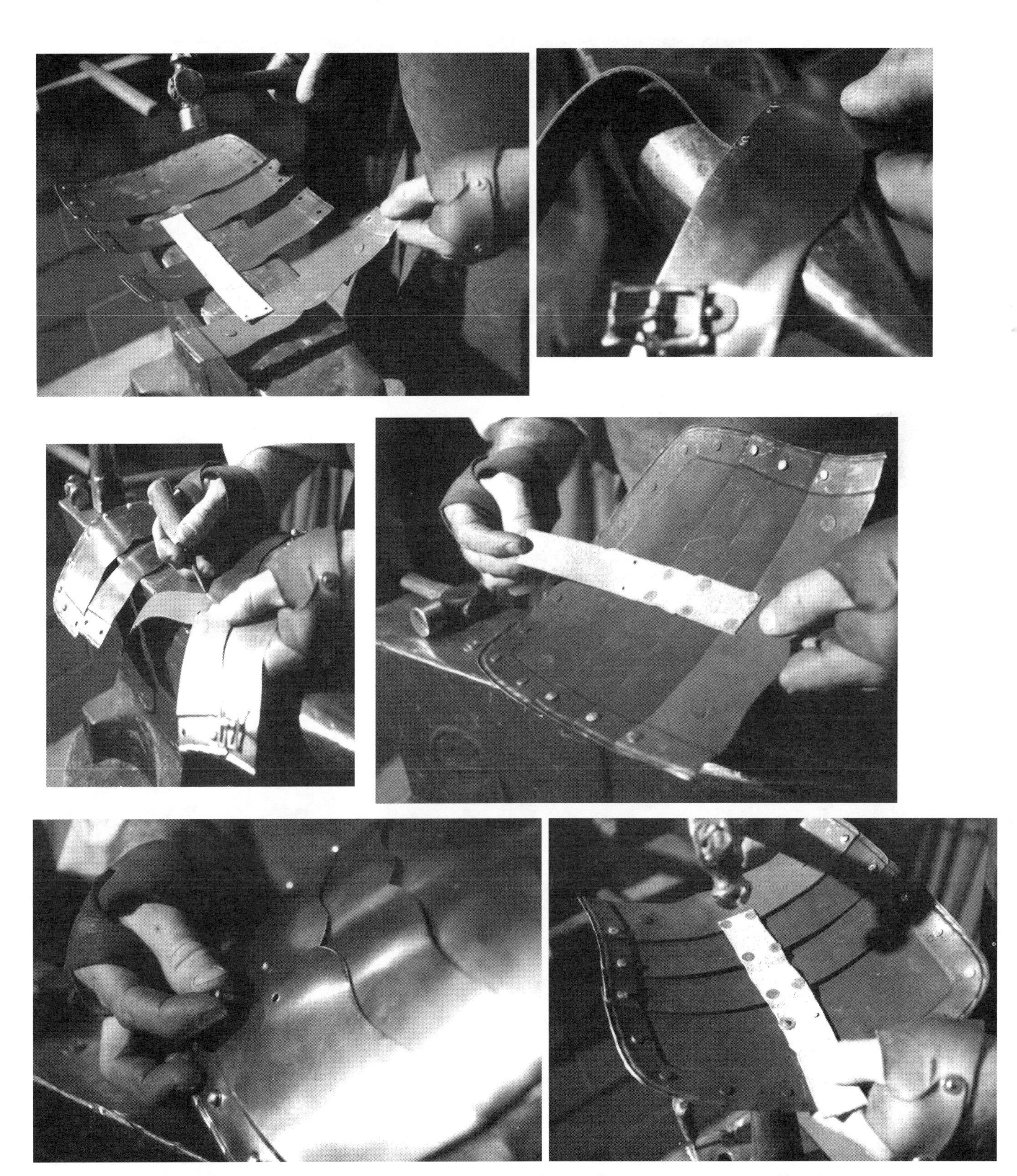

Laminated pieces were riveted together to become tassets. Originally these were mini shields, buckled to the fauld as extra protection for the legs. Here they are attached by buckles and belts, using decorative floral plates under the rivets.

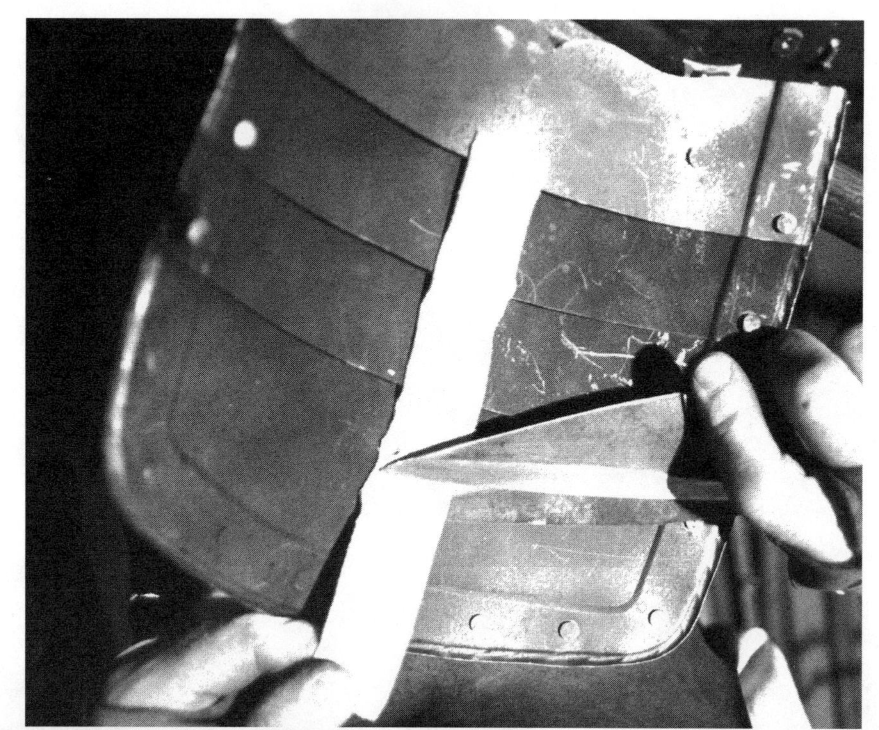

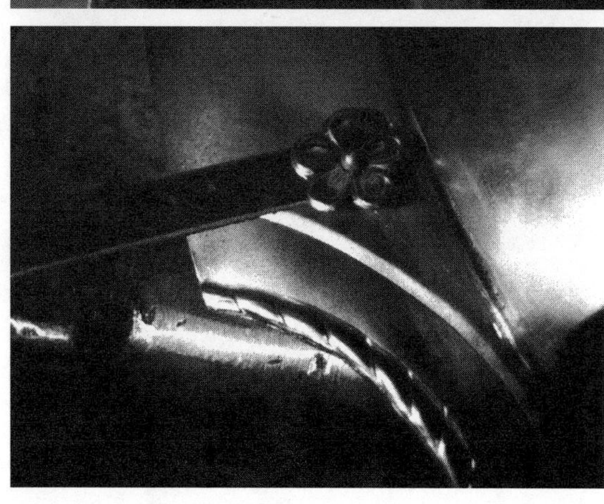

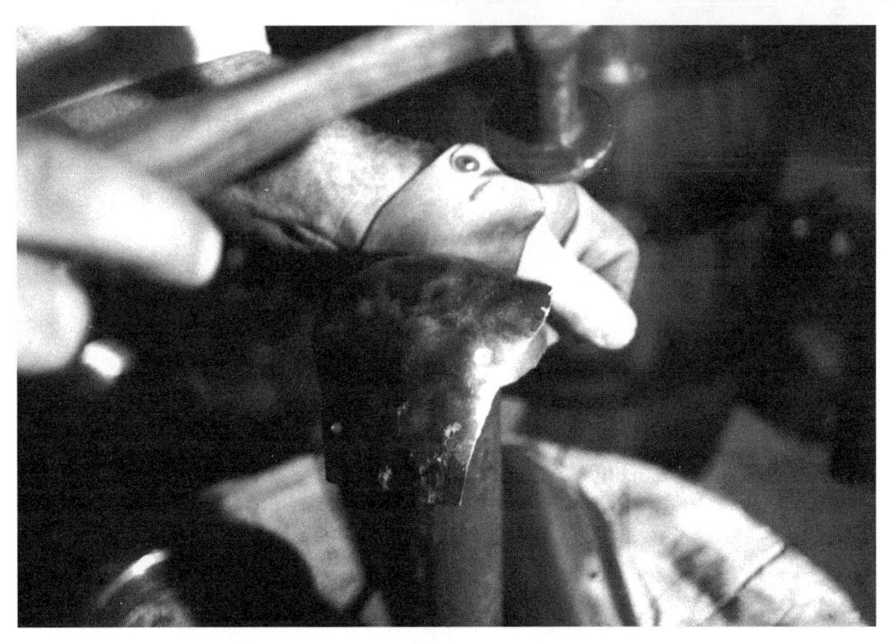

The elbow cop and inner fan are forged, then picked and filed to completion.

Pick and file.

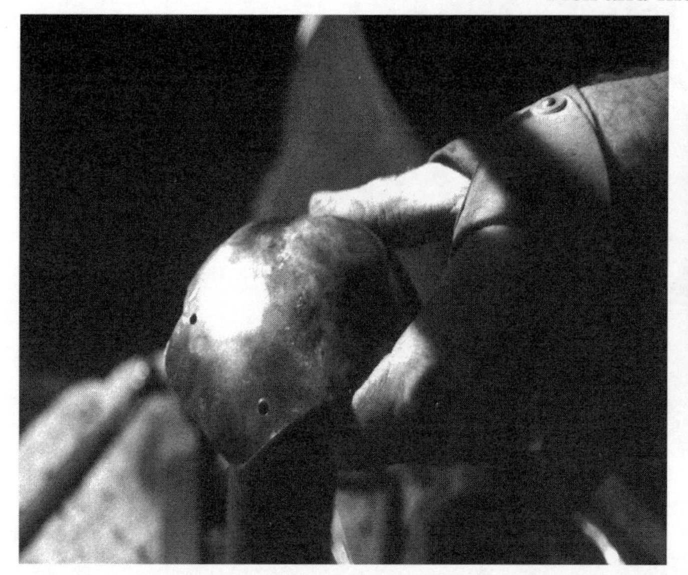

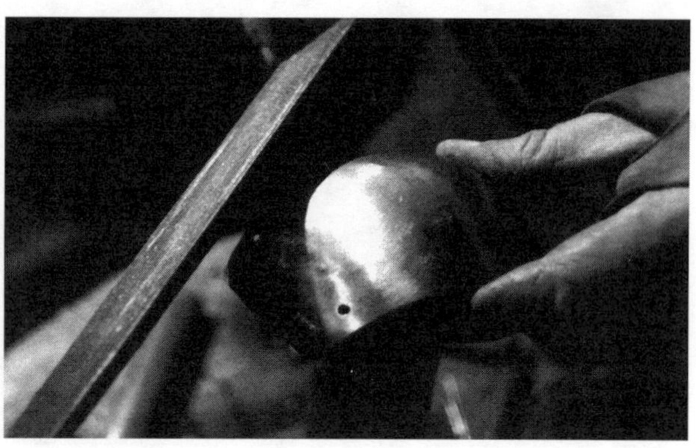

Forging the inner wing.

The elbow cop is then rolled, roped, and drop ledged to complete the homogeneous look.

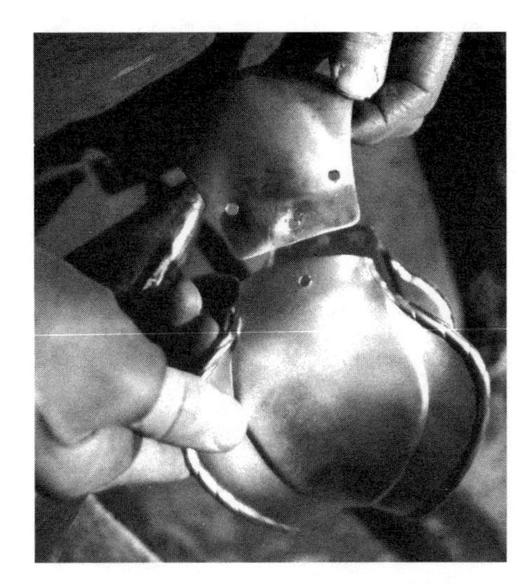

The inside wing is attached to the elbow cop.

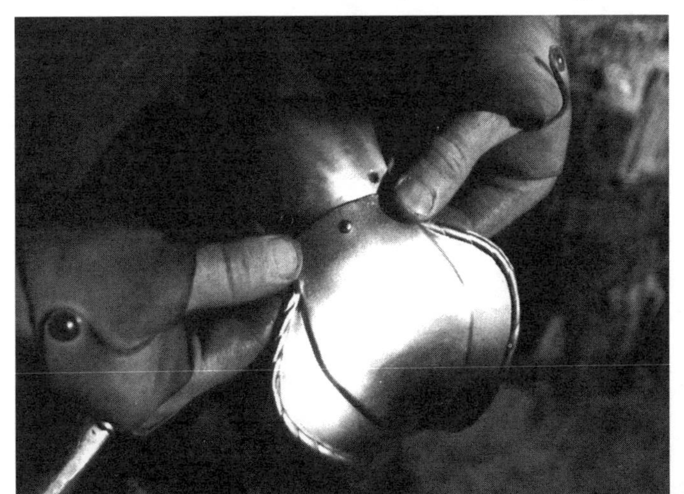

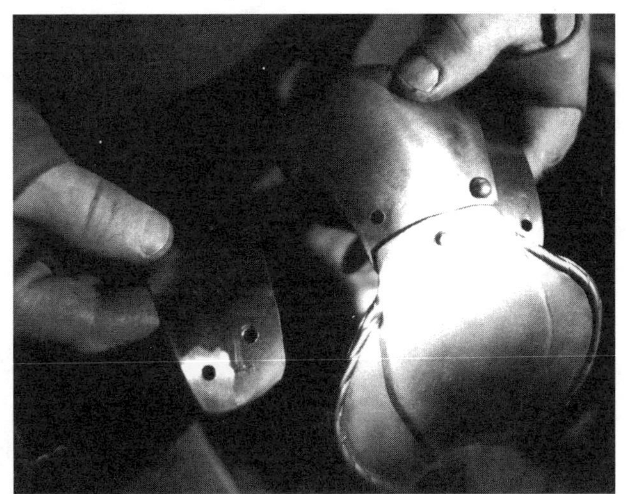

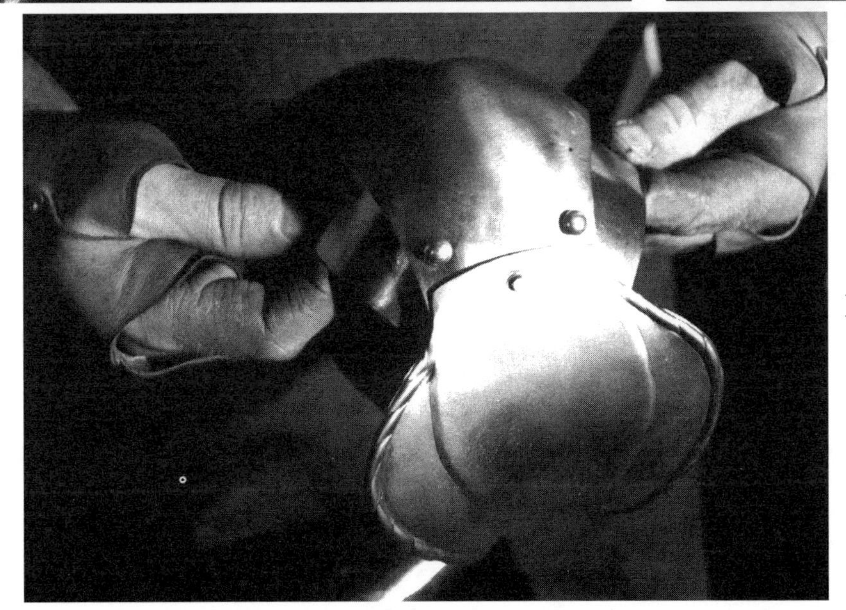

Lames are attached for articulation.

The armourer's mark shown here, again, was used to identify who made the piece. Several "armour guilds" were formed because of the necessity to regulate quality. Sometimes, copies of a popular armour piece were duplicated by lesser armourers, then passed off as if made by a famous craftsman. Soon it was necessary to have the city and guild marks on the armour as well, just to get the customer's approval.

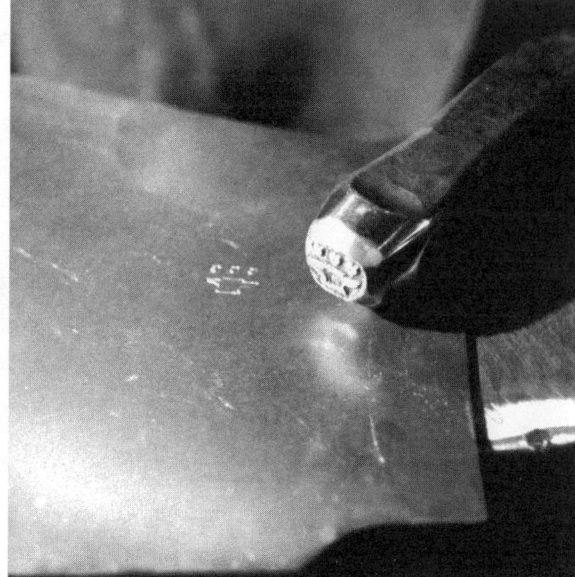

The hinges are riveted and formed on to the vambraces.

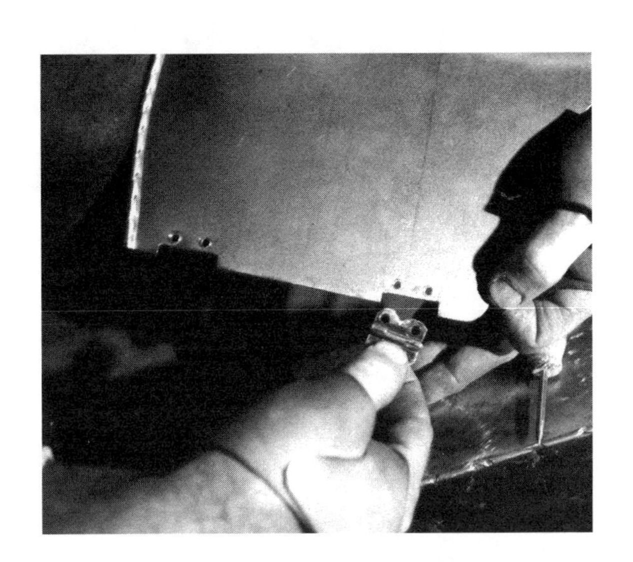

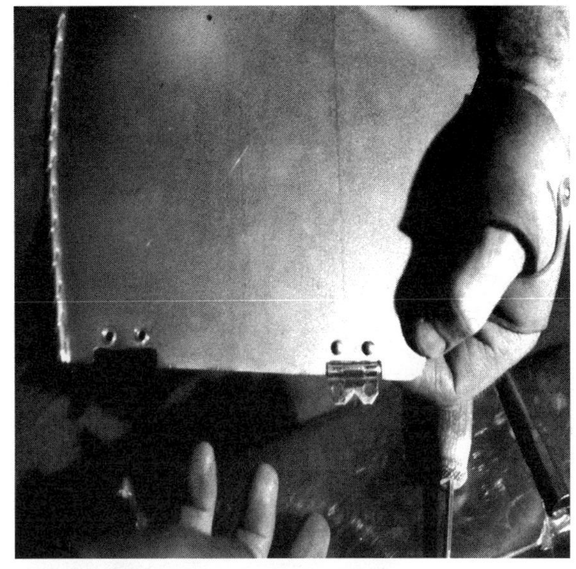

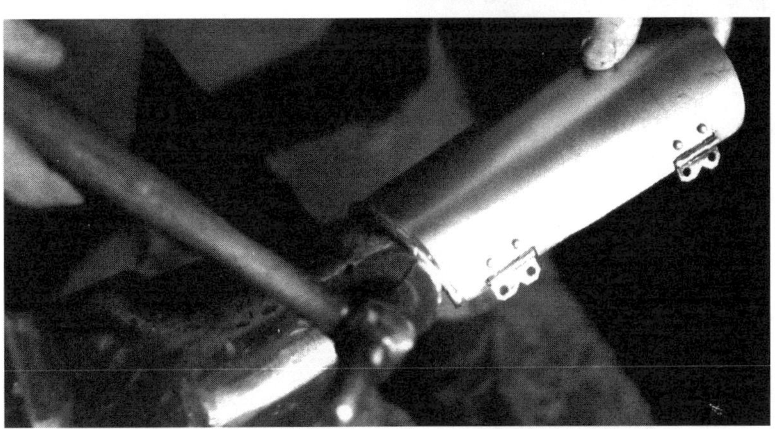

Using the same system as the greaves, the vambraces are riveted and pins are attached. Then the vambraces are attached to the elbow cops.

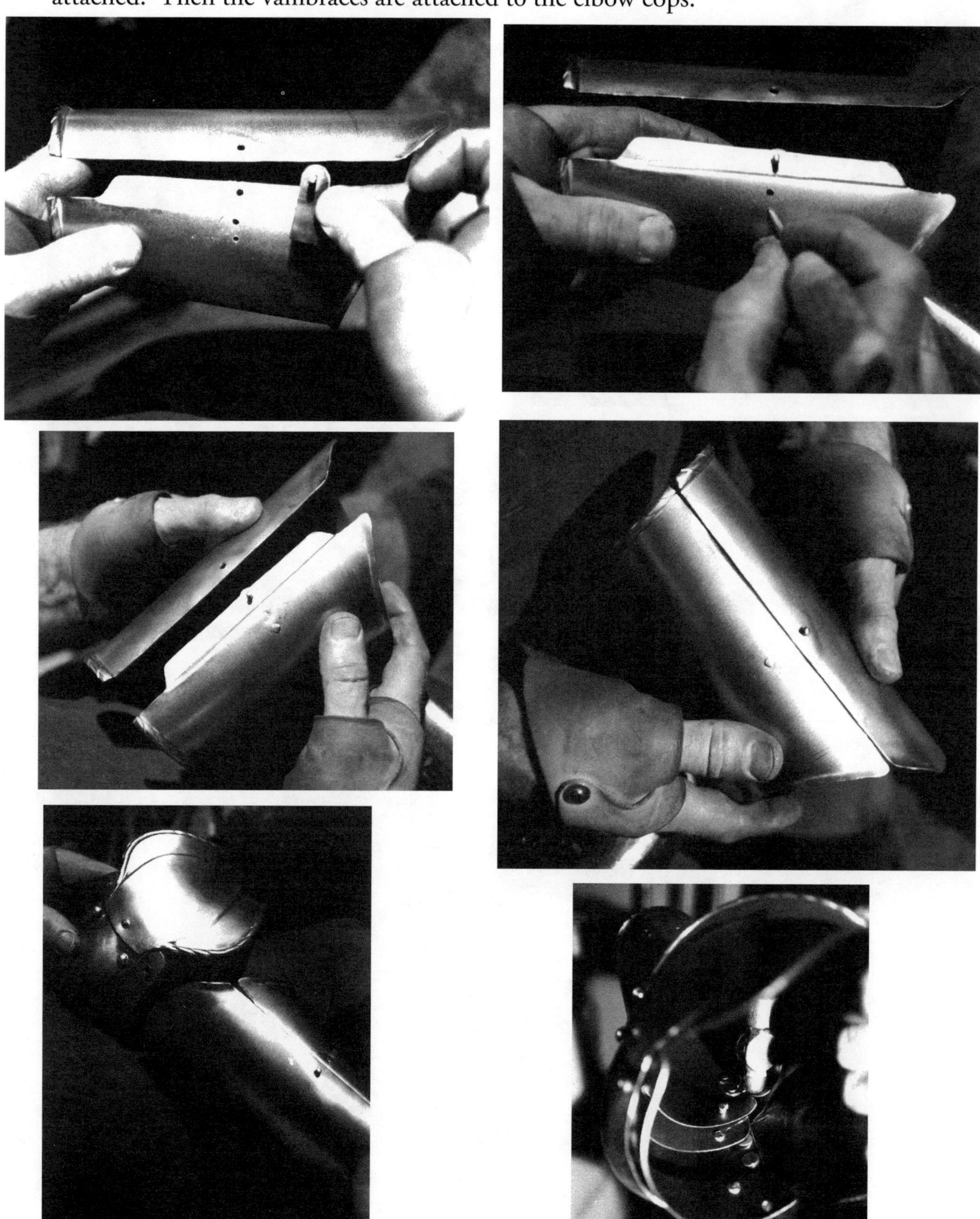

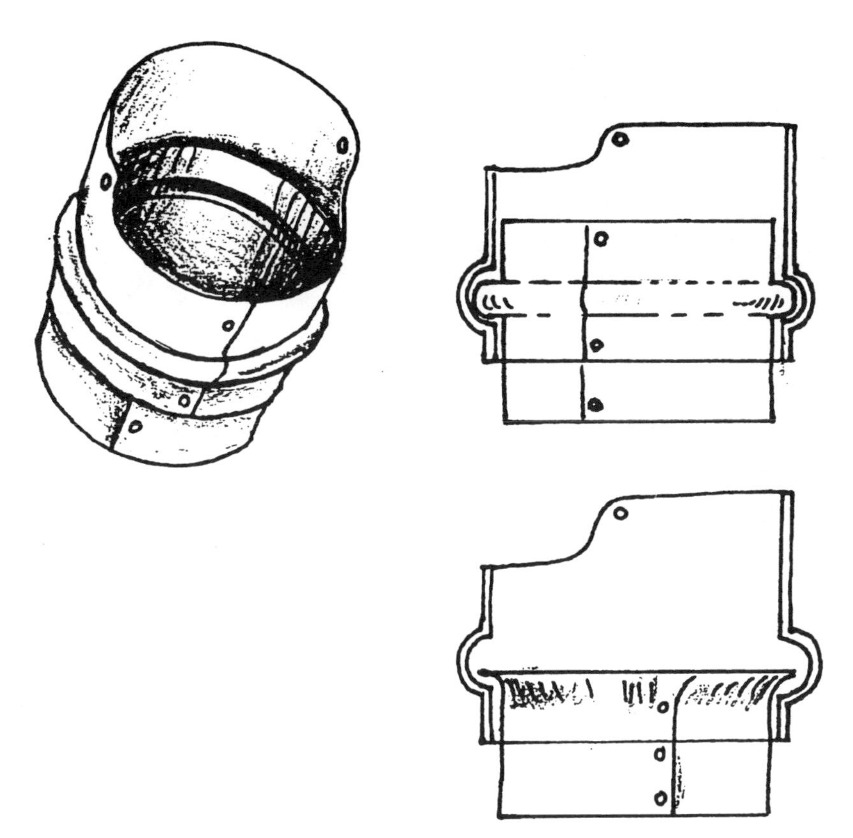

We decided to use one of these well known turn pin systems for the rerebrace. Movement like this was needed for the arm to function properly. However, if the rerebrace was hit or damaged and the cylinder was not completely circular, it would cease to function properly.

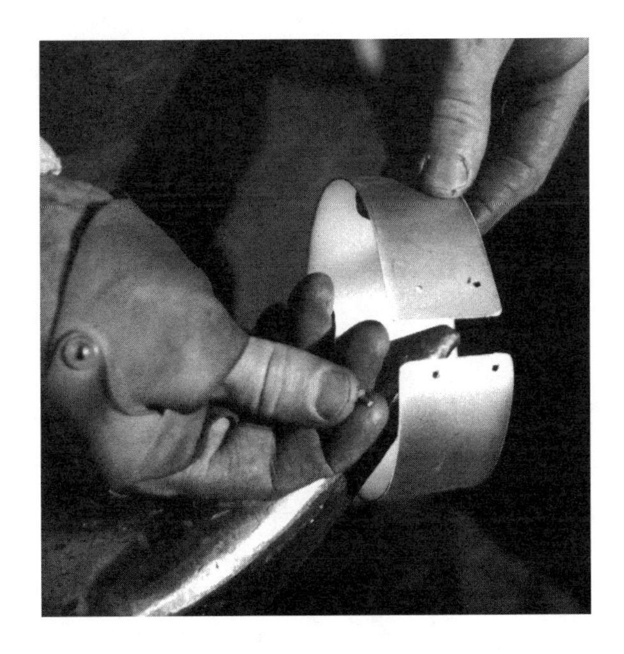

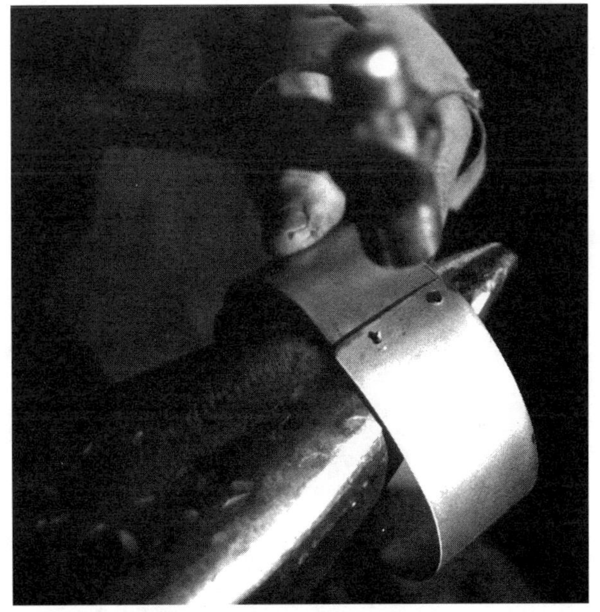

The rerebrace is finished, then attached to the elbow cop and vambrace.

As the same as most armour, the left side of any suit is reinforced more than the right side, because everybody throughout Europe was taught and encouraged to be right-handed. It was thought left-handed people were guided by the devil.

Knights needed more maneuverability with their right arm. All sword blows and attacks were directed to the left side of the body.

By the time full plate was used by knights, shields were seldom used because they were wearing their shields, or would have reinforced pieces attached to their arms: Either shoulders or large elbow cops. On our model, we have a haute-piece attached to the left shoulder pauldron.

Haute piece for left side usually.

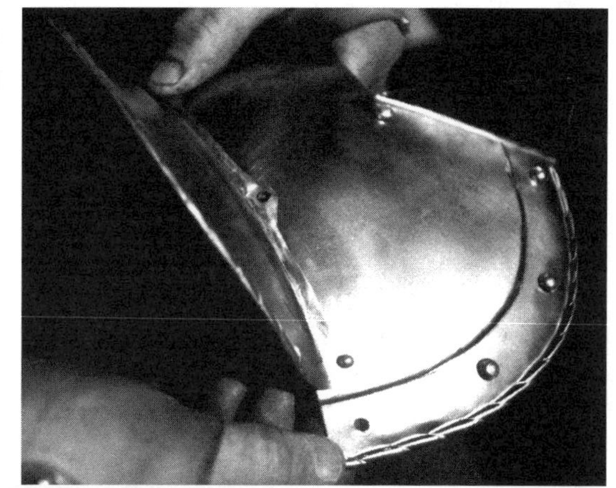

Pivoting lames.

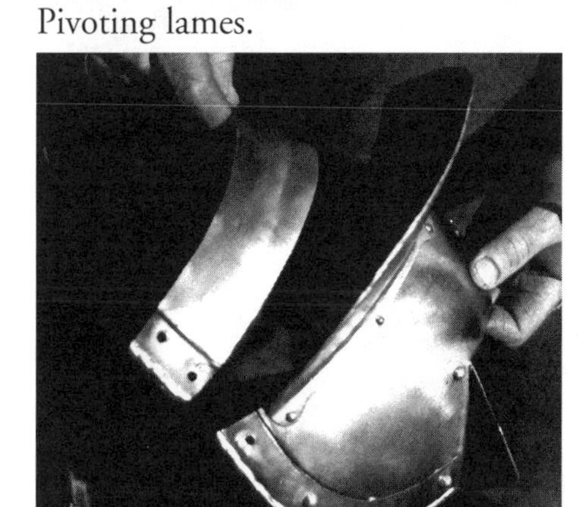

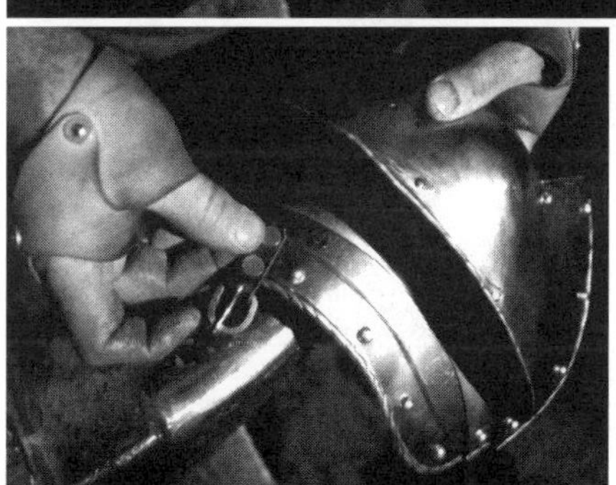

Pin or buckle suspension systems.

Historically, upper arm lames were also attached to the pauldrons.

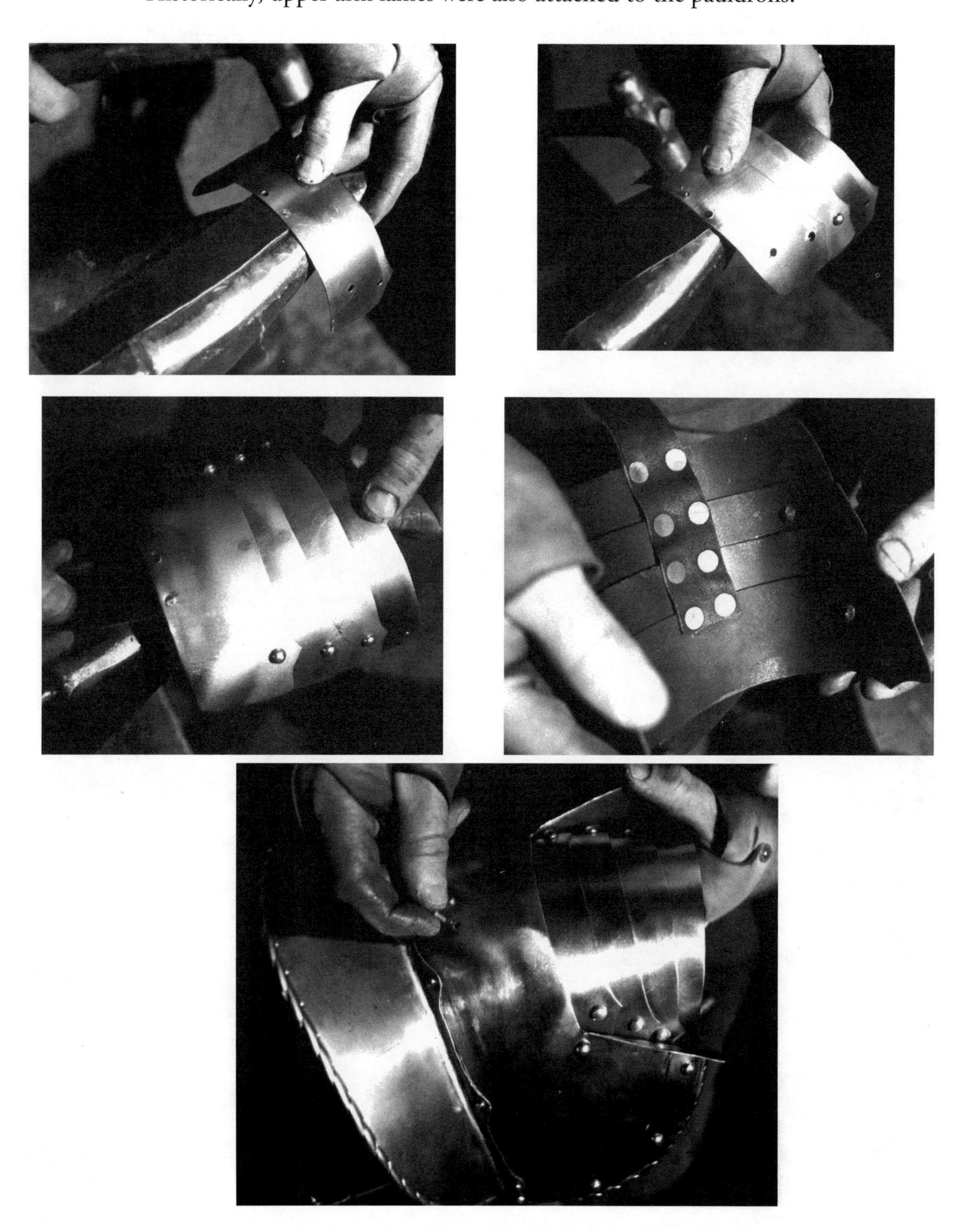

The shoulder pauldron is then riveted to the turn pin of the rerebrace.

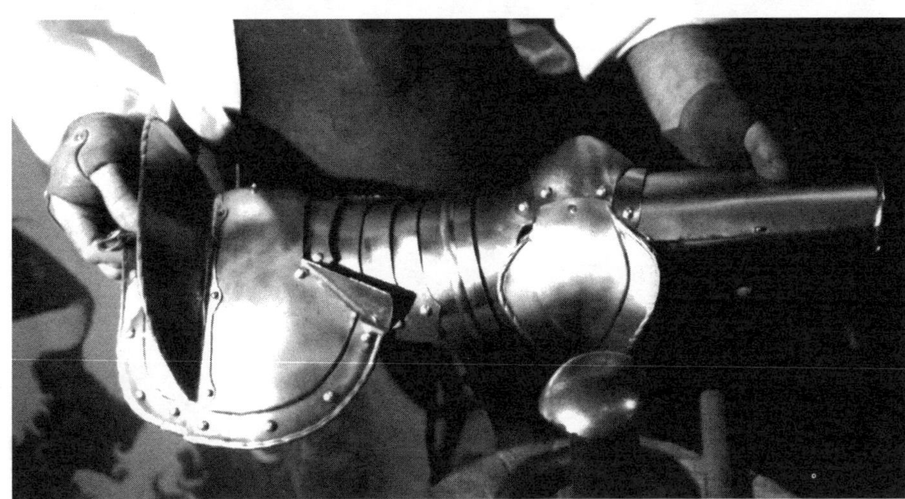

Gauntlets were the piece of armour that had to have complete mobility and they usually were the most complex for movable pieces. Shown are several laminations and articulated thumb pieces.

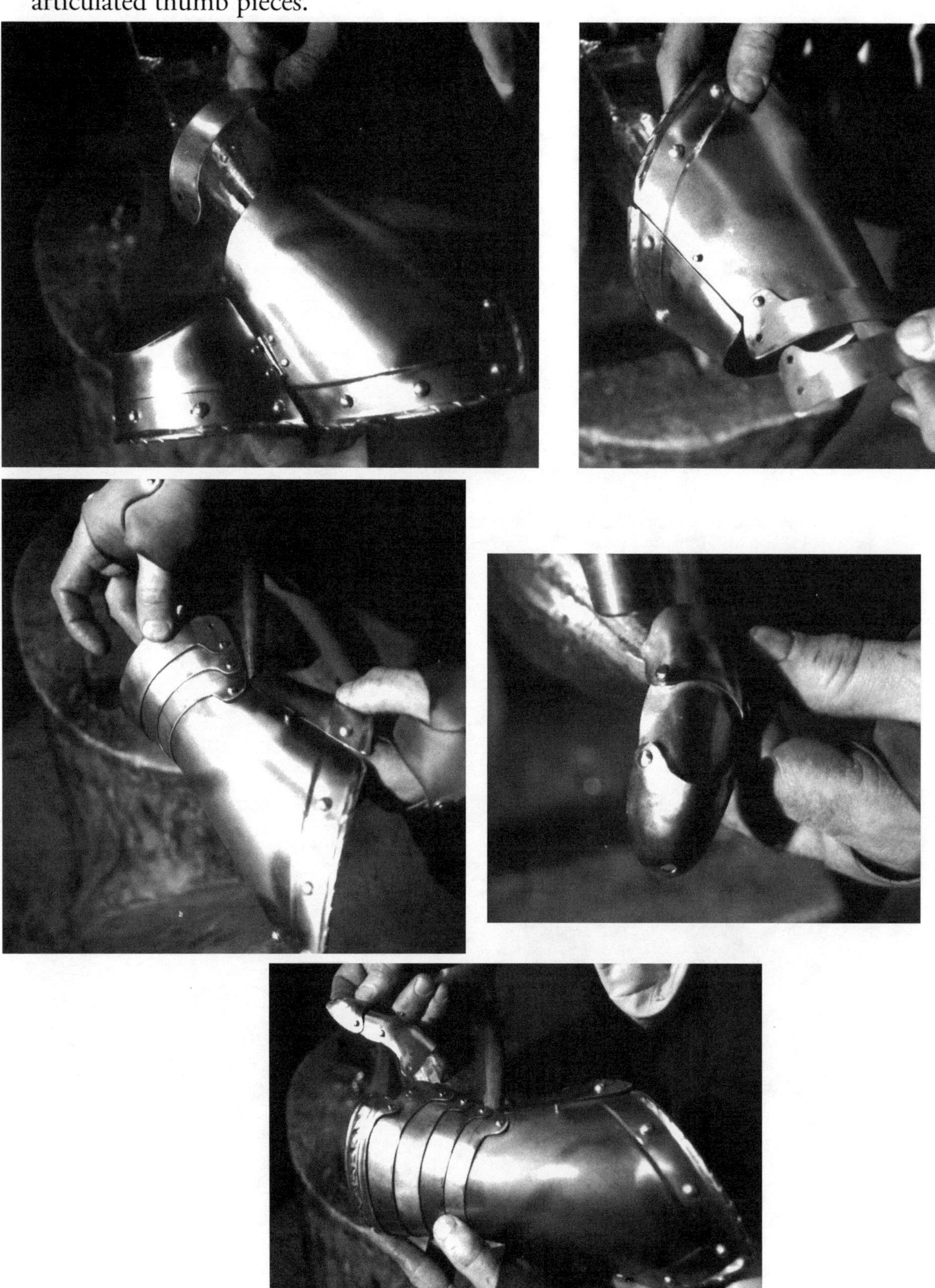

Each finger piece was historically handmade. It was filed, then had a hole punched into it, then it was attached to a leather strip. Several pieces were attached to each leather strip, to create the length of a finger. These leather strips were then riveted to the knuckle piece.

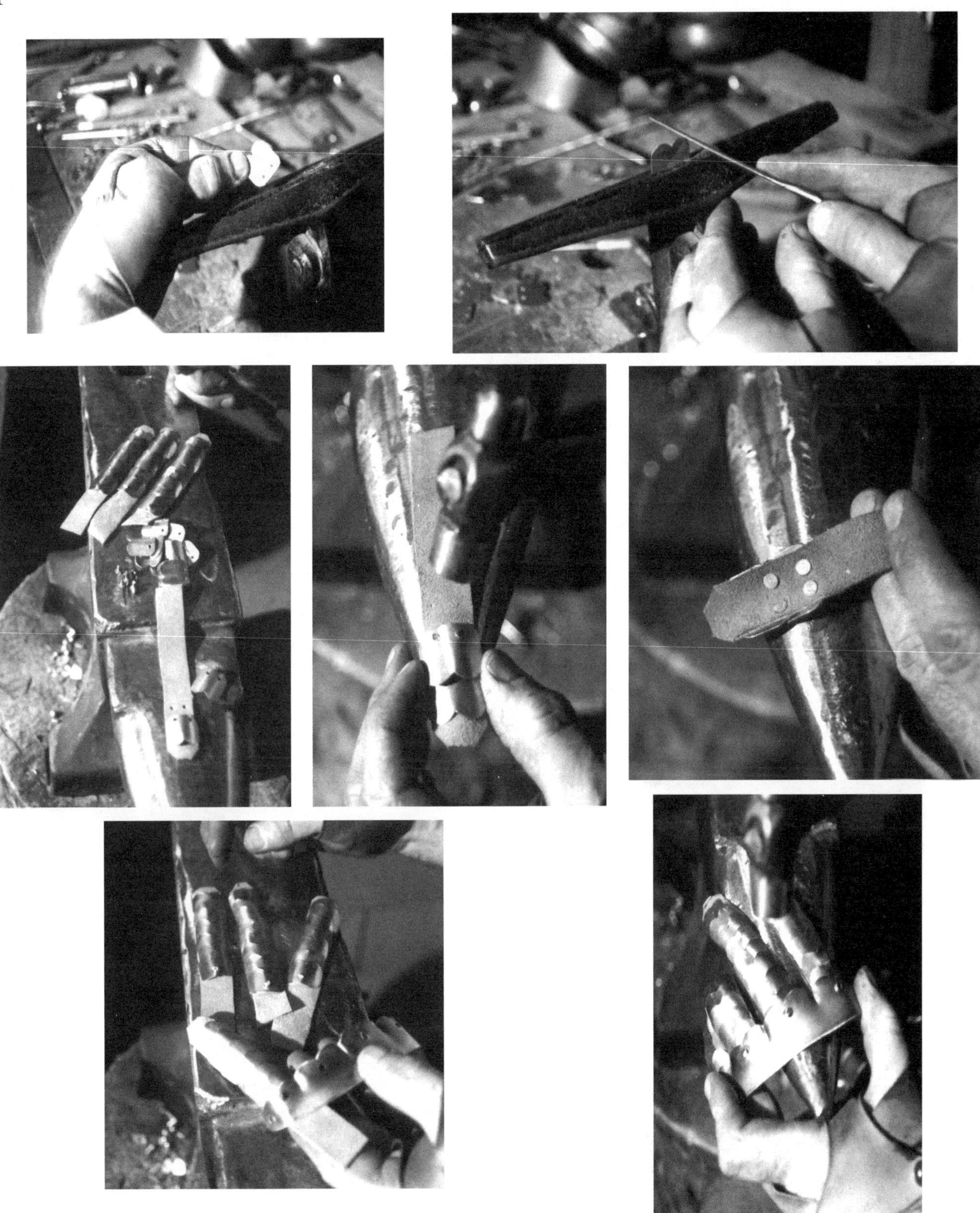

A leather glove was historically riveted to the steel part of the gauntlet. The leather strips with finger pieces attached were first glued, then sewn to the gloves. If the glove became worn out, which was often, it could be replaced by a new glove. The gauntlet usually outlasted the glove. In museums today, you can see gauntlets on original suits with the gloves long gone.

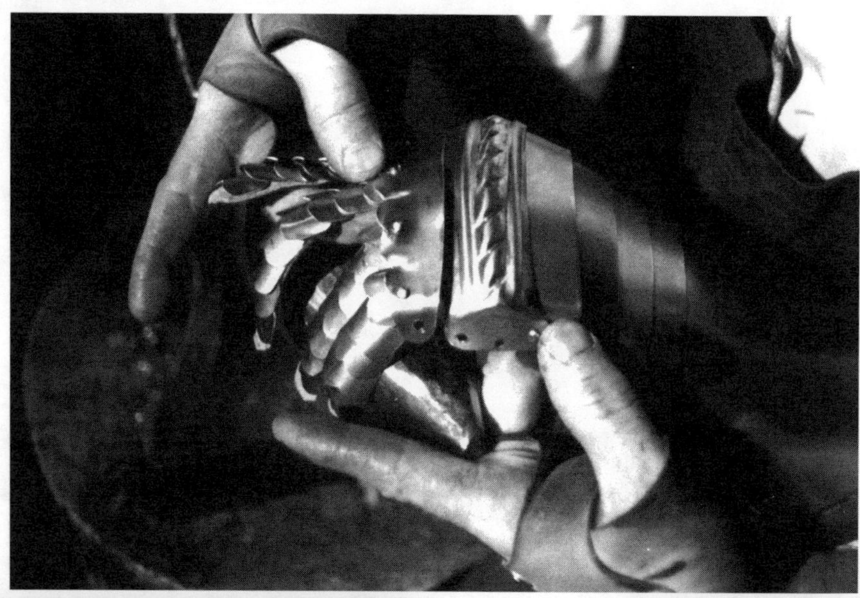

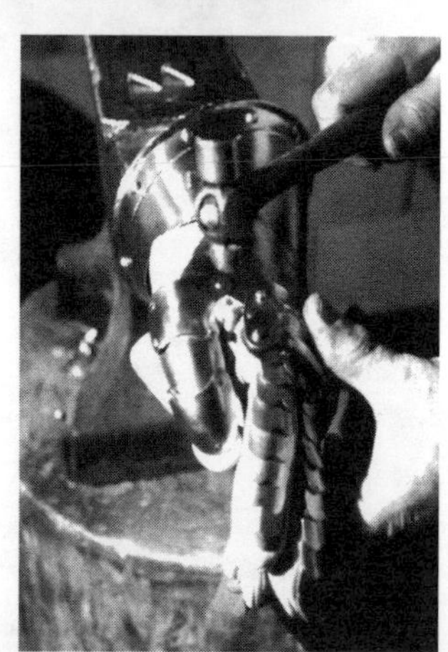

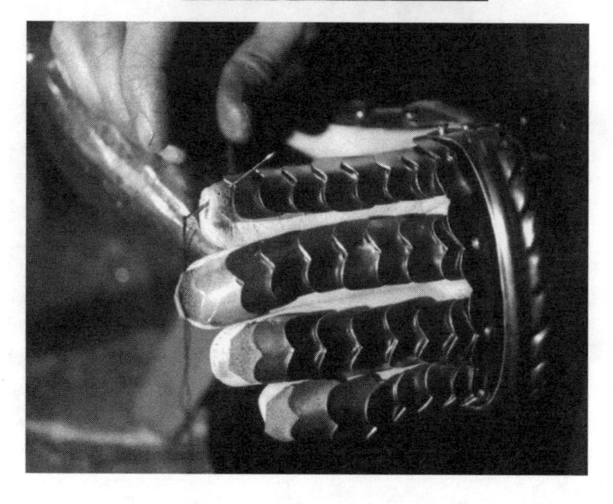

As early as 700 A.D., chainmail was used as a primary body defense. Probably invented by the Celts, it was introduced to the Romans when they campaigned in Britain.

Chainmail was fairly easy to make and provided good protection...providing the links were riveted together. It was used throughout medieval history. By the 16th century, chainmail was used as a complementary armour to plate armour.

This is an example of a basic rolling machine. Historically, wire would be turned around a rod like this to make a spring shaped coil, cut off, then cut into individual rings.

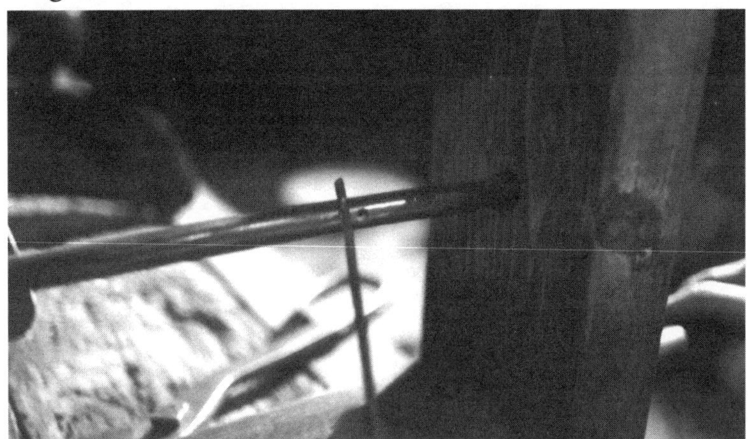

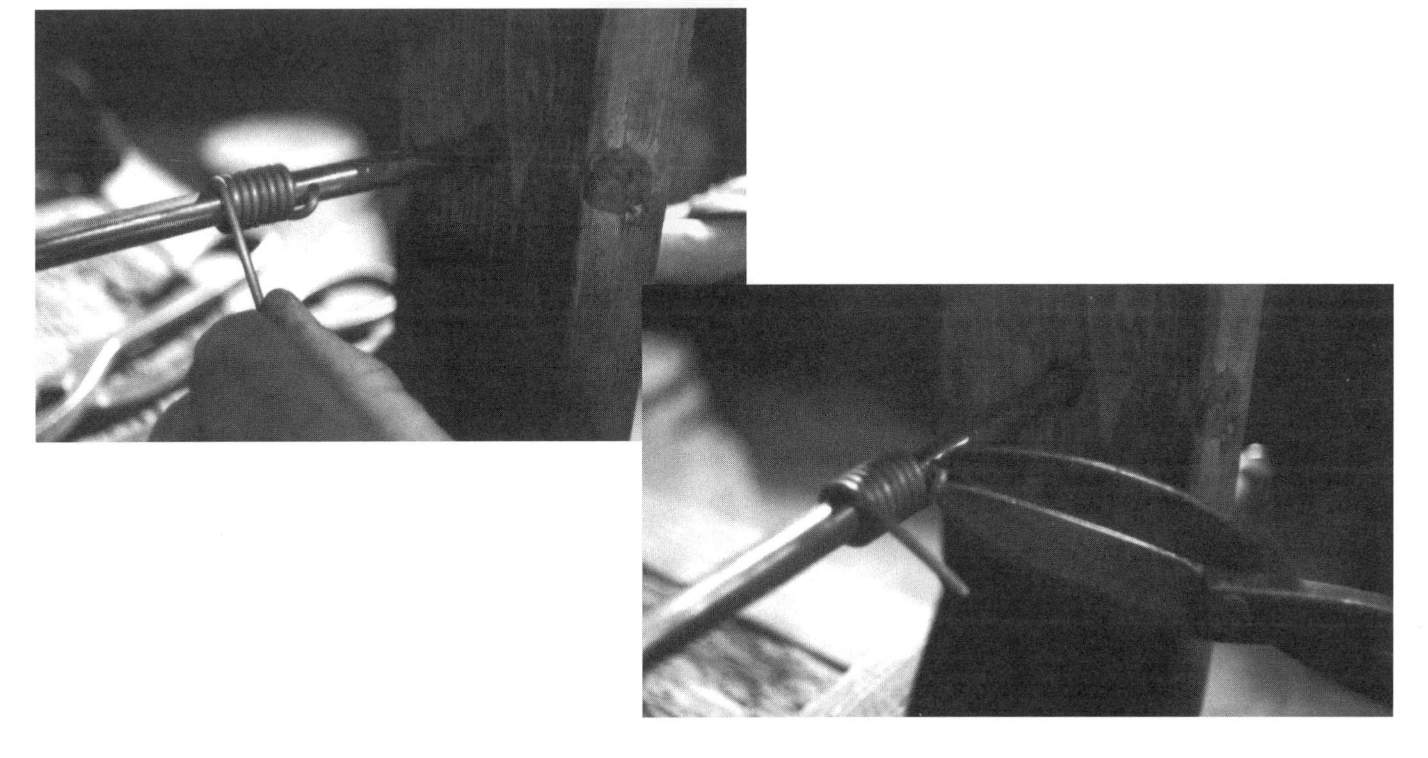

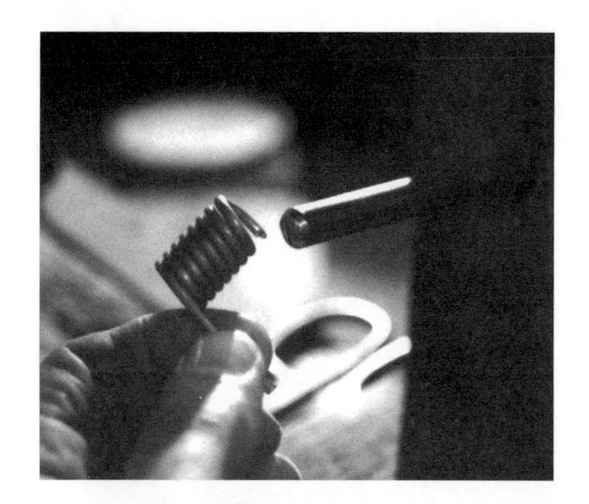

Chainmail in the 16th century was usually a separate business from the amourer. The amourer would commission a piece for his customer.

Often links were flattened in the process of preparing it for punching the hole for the rivet.

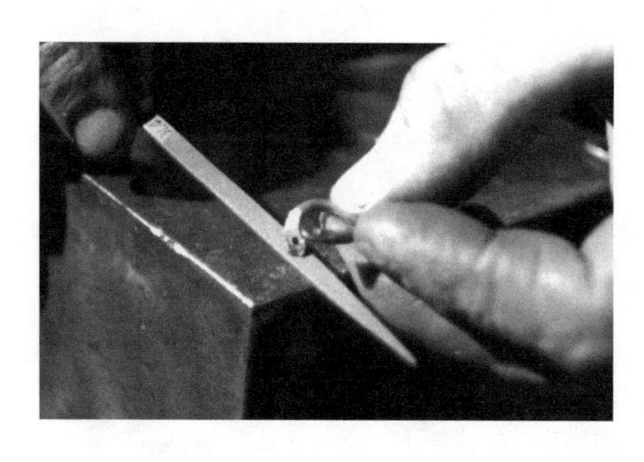

The links are filed and prepared to attach to the other riveted links. There were several different ways to attach the two ends, but we are using a simple pin.

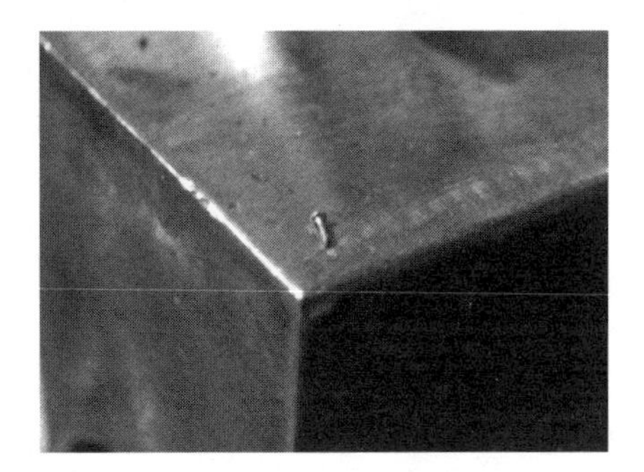

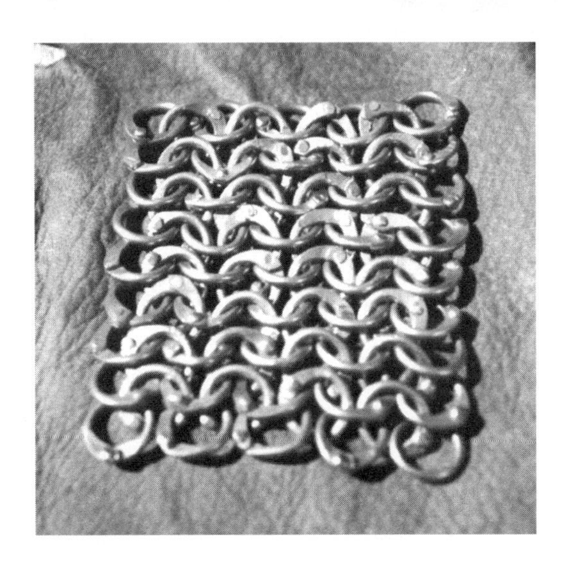

A chainmail skirt is made to be worn under the breastplate and over the top of the legs.

Helmet: After the initial forging, the final shaping and clean-up would have historically been done cold on steel stakes, with a planishing hammer and different files.

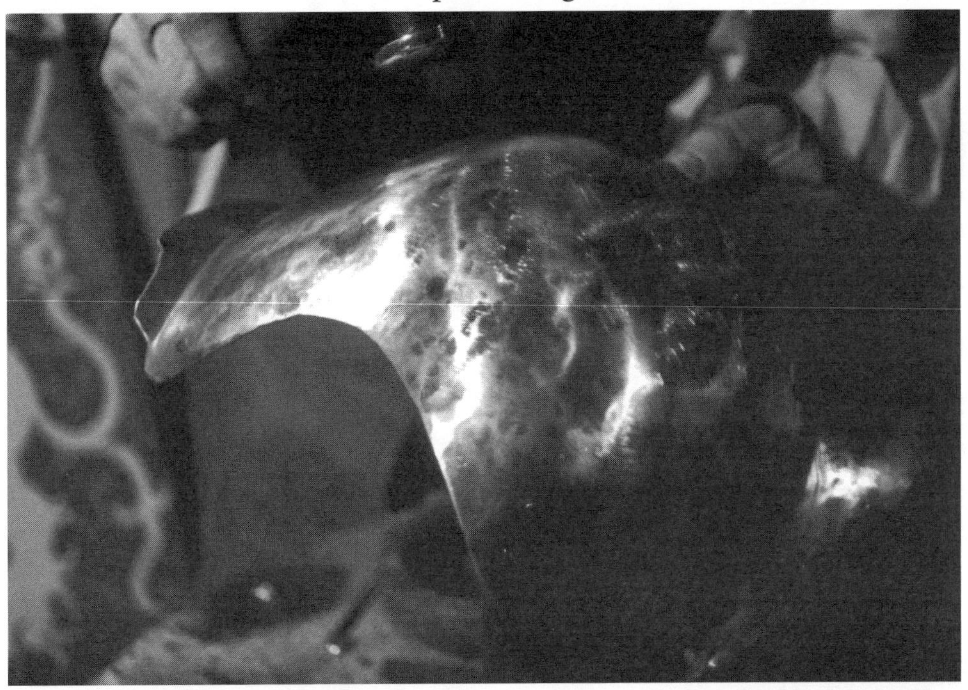

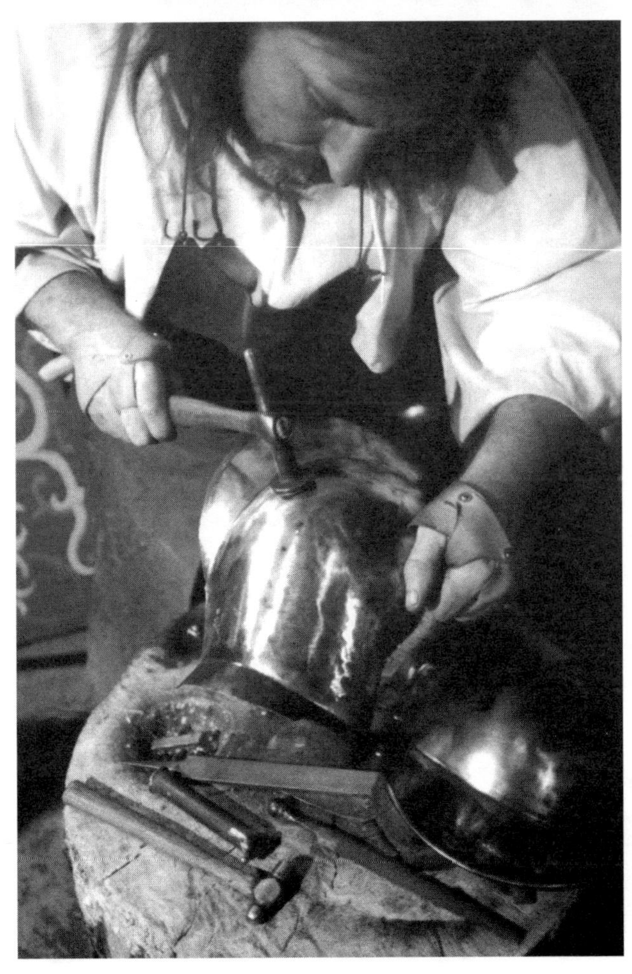

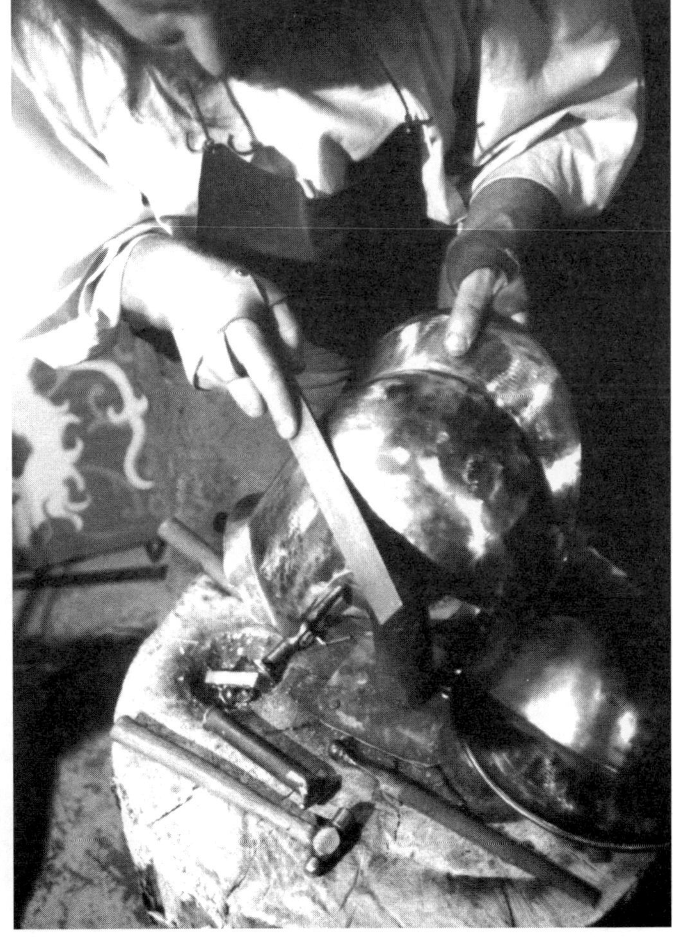

Most close helmets were historically made in one piece. Some were made in two pieces. These halves are attached by rivets, then the top is rolled over and crimped to hold the comb together.

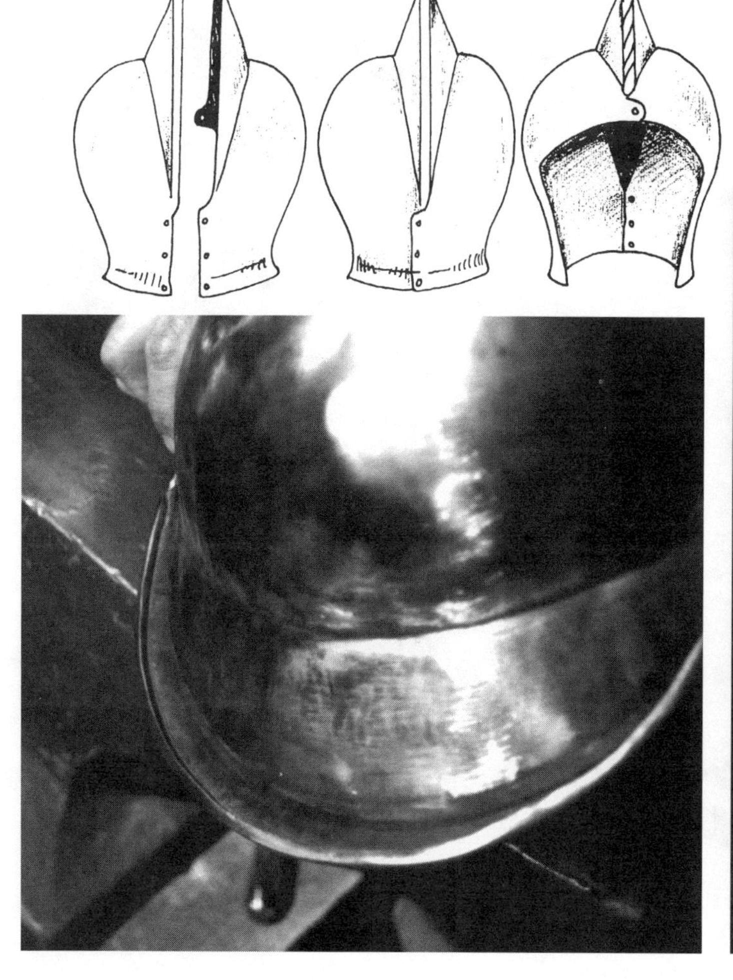

To complete the homogeneous look of all pieces, the top is given a rope finish, this time by filing it.

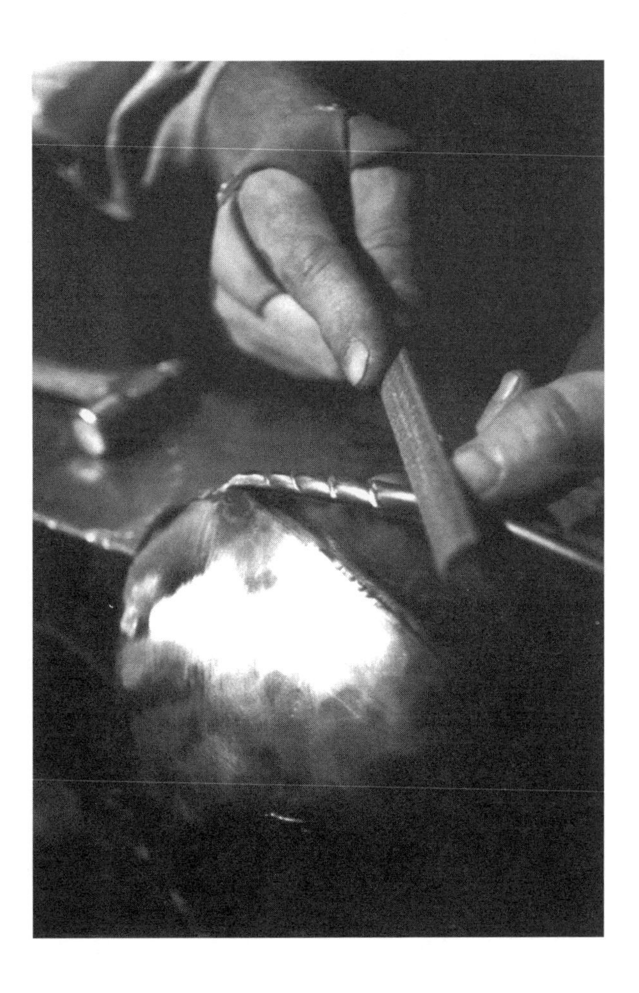

The helmet tops are then forge-welded together, so there is no visible seam. To do this, the temperature of the metal must be yellow hot, then hammered together. This is done to both the front and back of the skull part of the helmet.

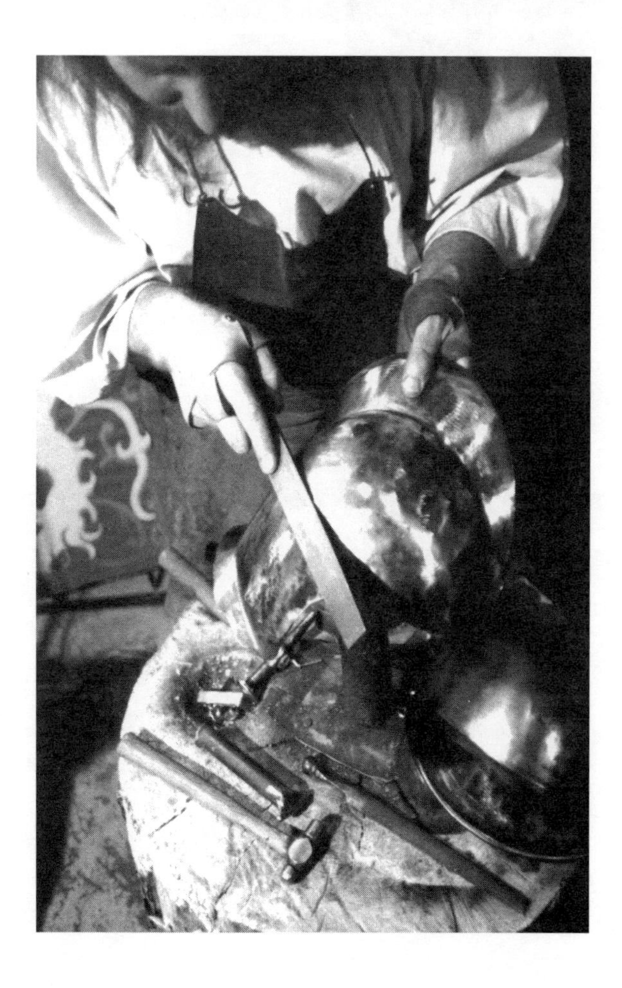

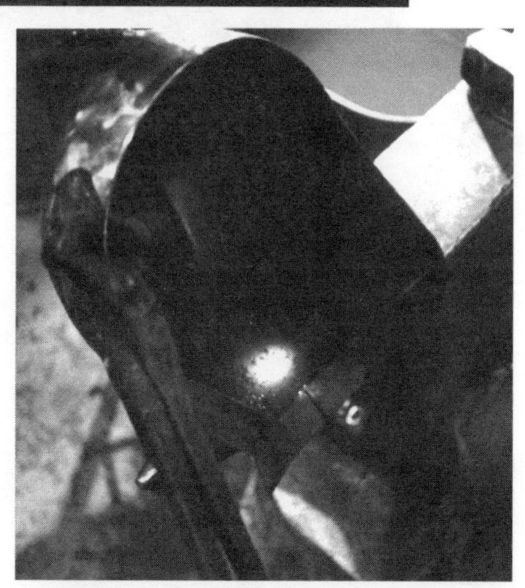

Ventail

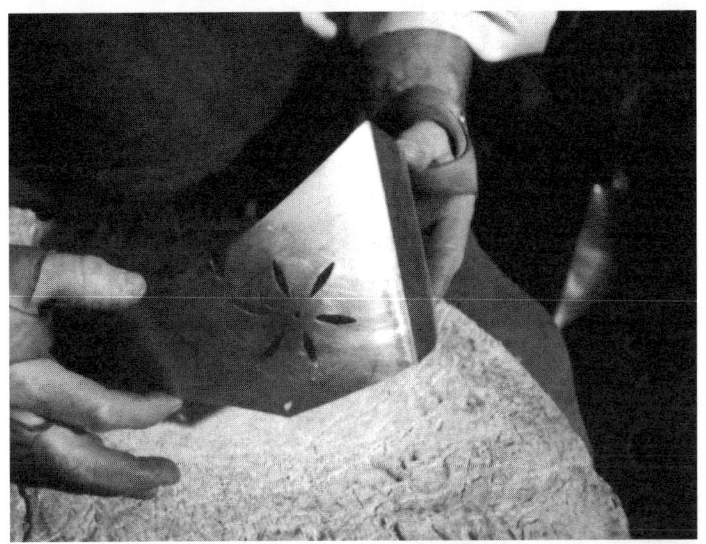

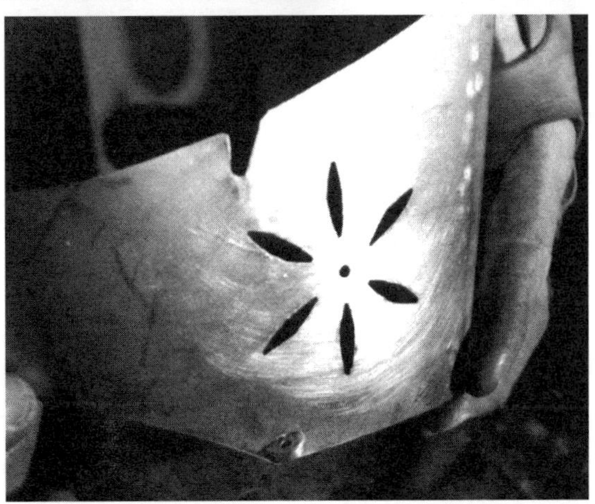

Visor

The eyes and other holes are punched out by using this basic technique. The lifting peg is then riveted on.

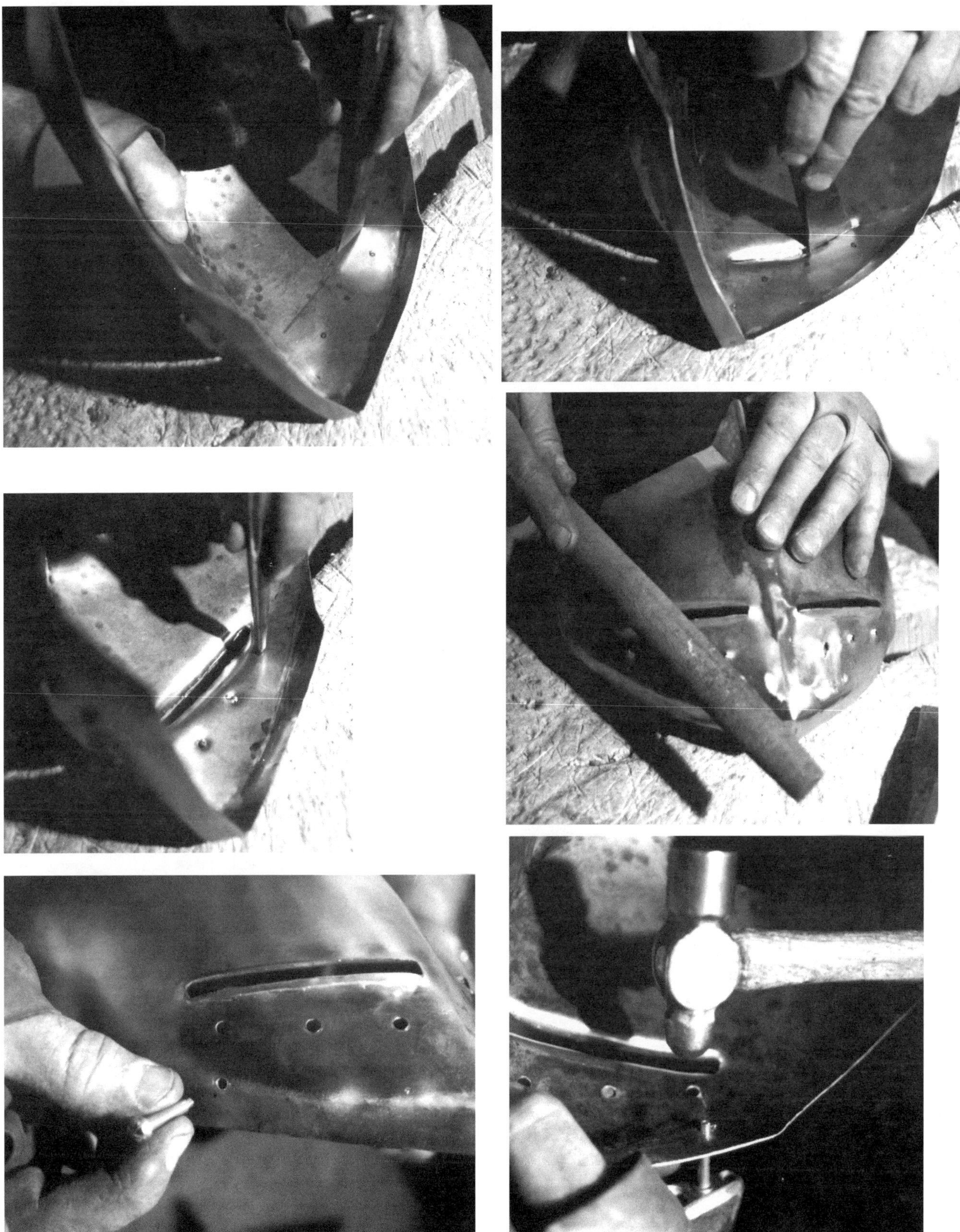

Now we start to fit all pieces of the front of the helmet together. The visor, ventail, bevor, and gorget are all connected, and they pivot on two large bolts and nuts, one on each side.

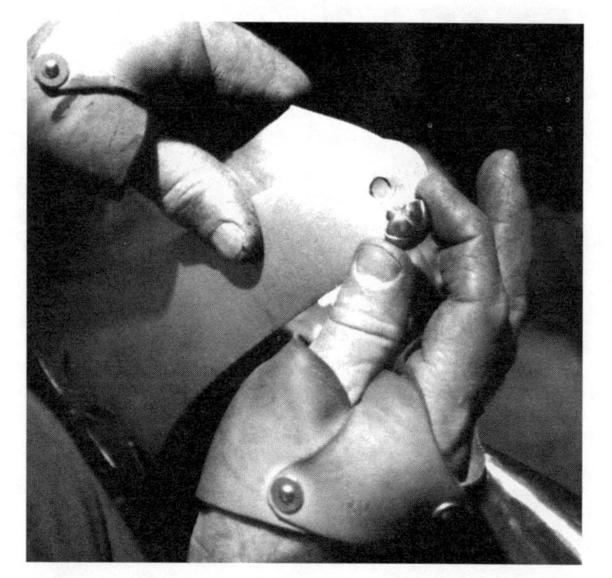

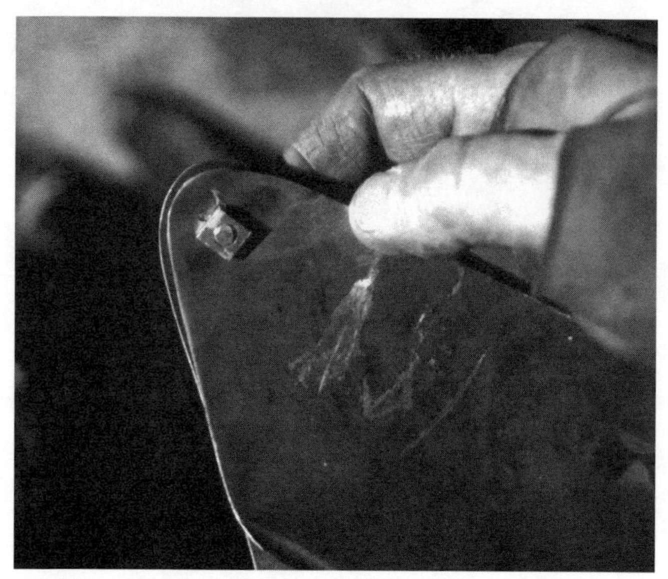

A hook-hole that will connect the front of the helmet to the skull part is riveted on.

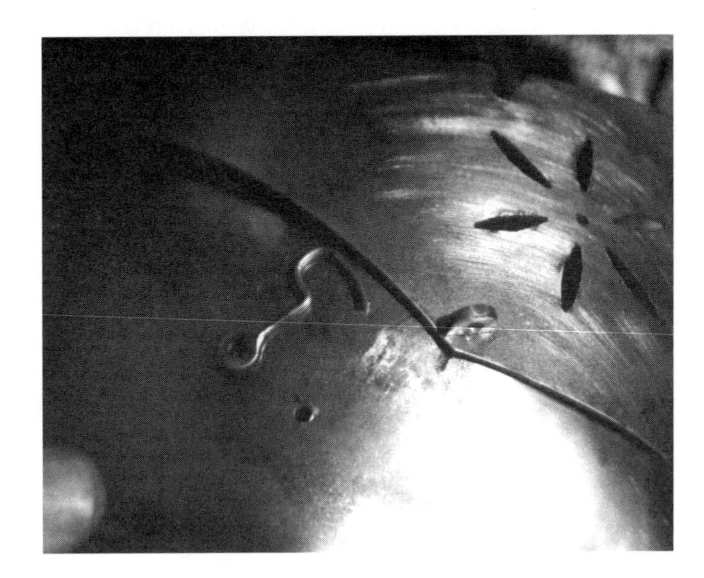

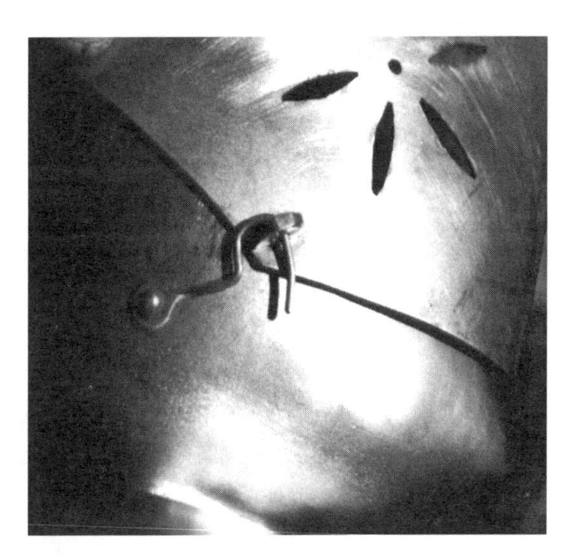

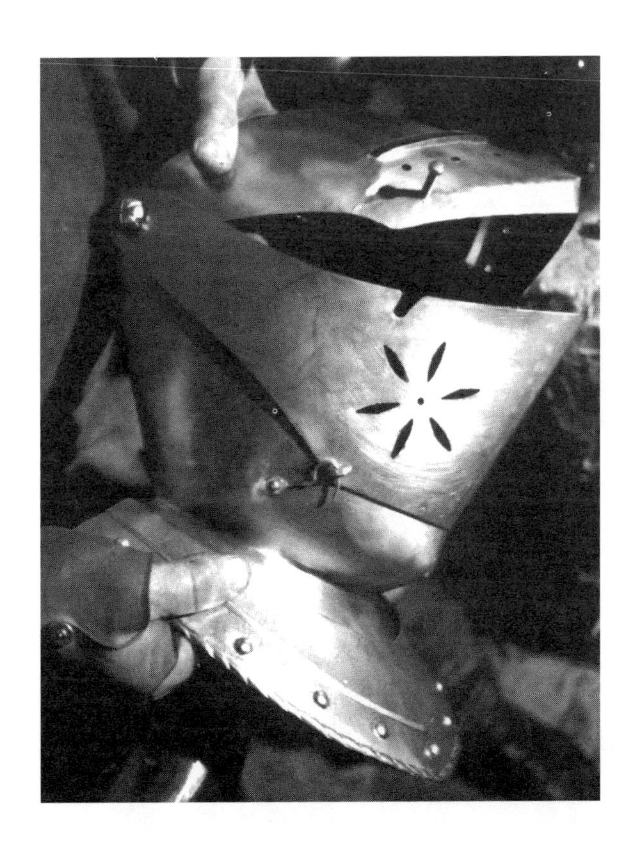

The plume holder was used to display the wearer's colors on the field, as well as on the tournament Eric. Ostrich feathers dyed several different colors were used. This holder is attached with rivets.

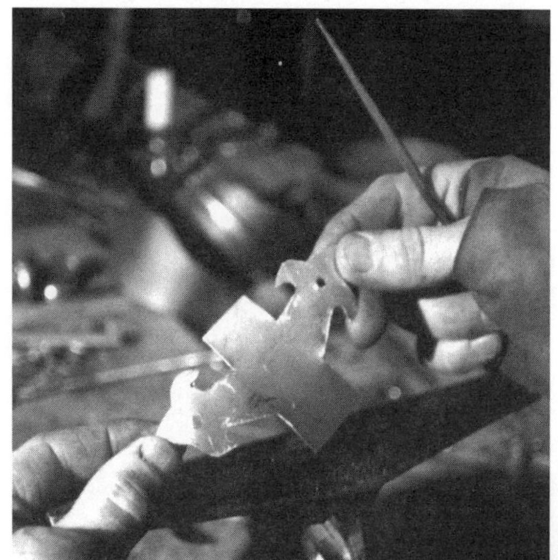

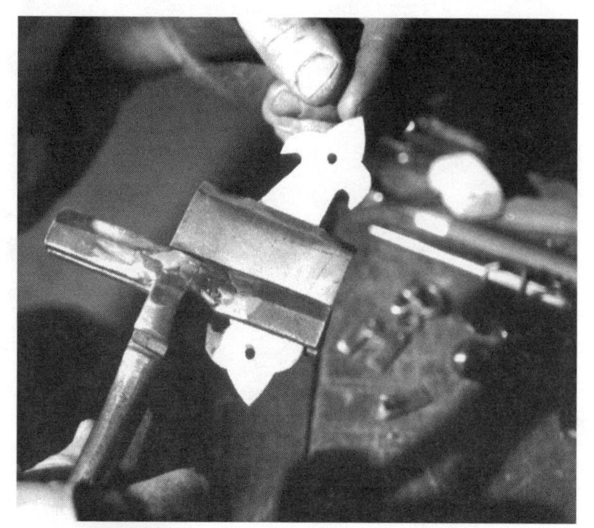

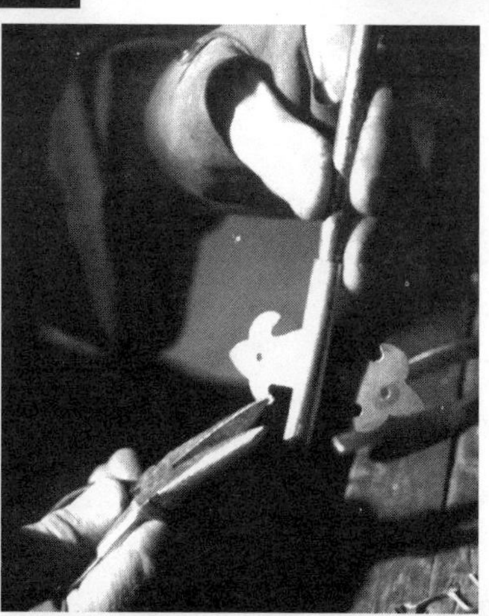

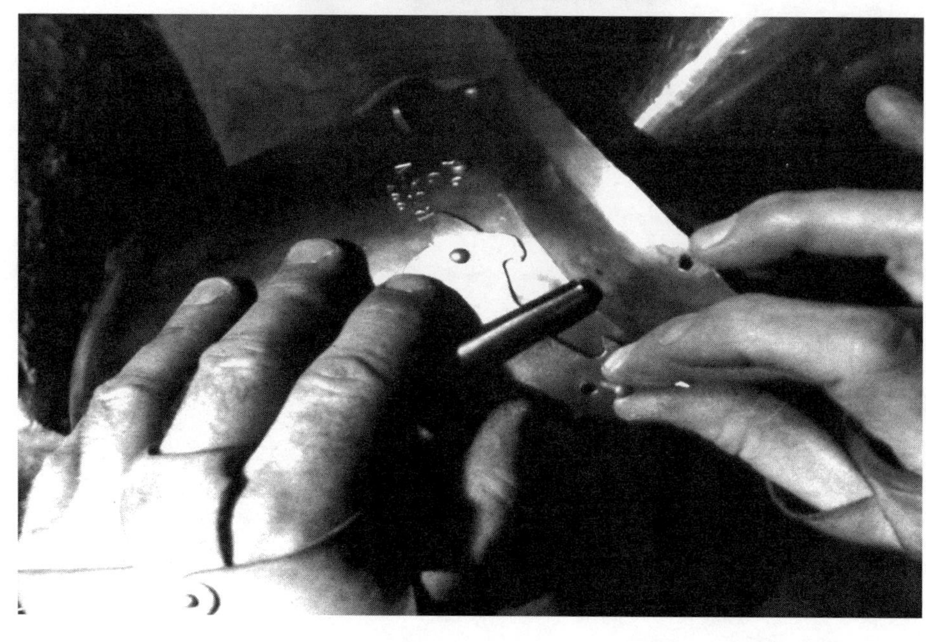

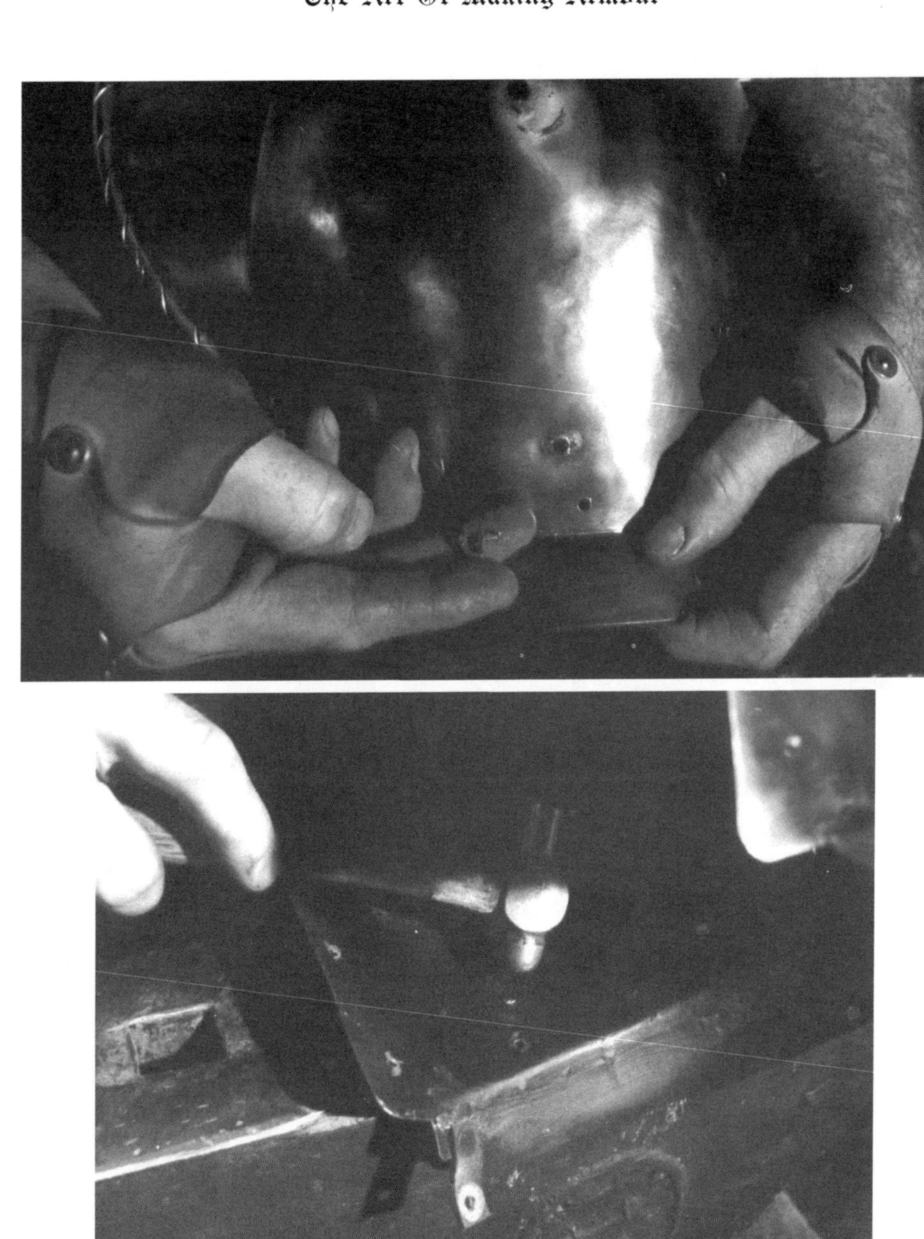

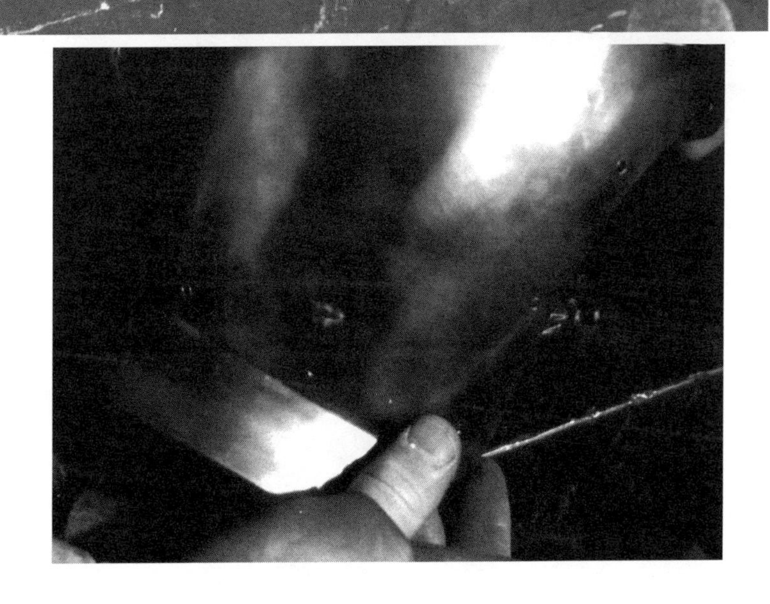

Helmets had liners attached to the inside of the helmets, usually made of leather or a strong material. They could also be stuffed with padding (like cloth or horsehair) at a later time if desired.

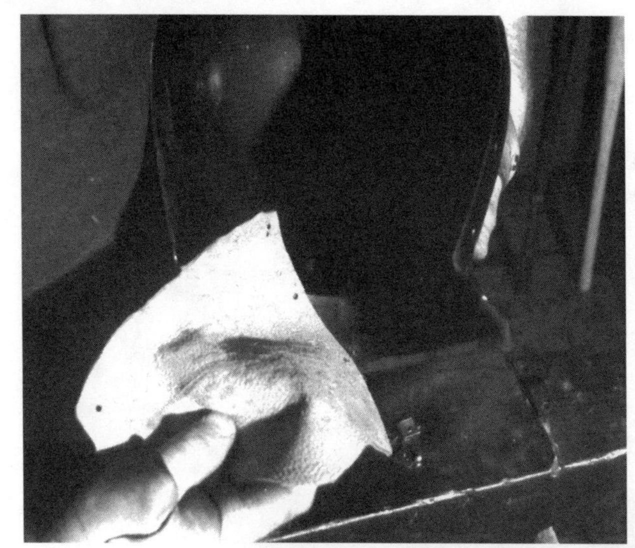

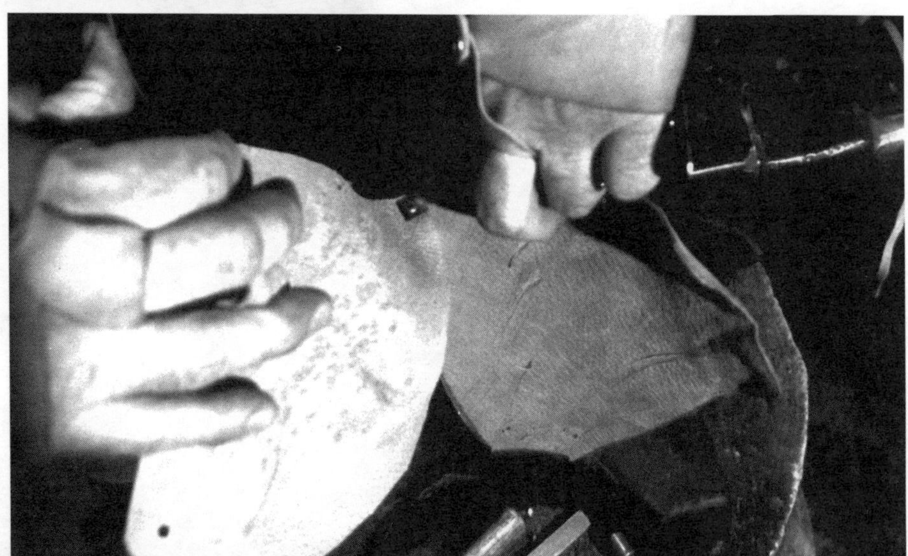

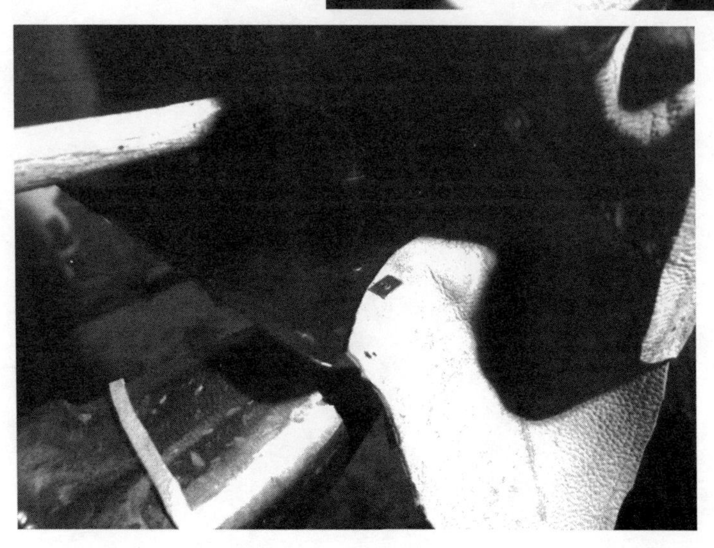

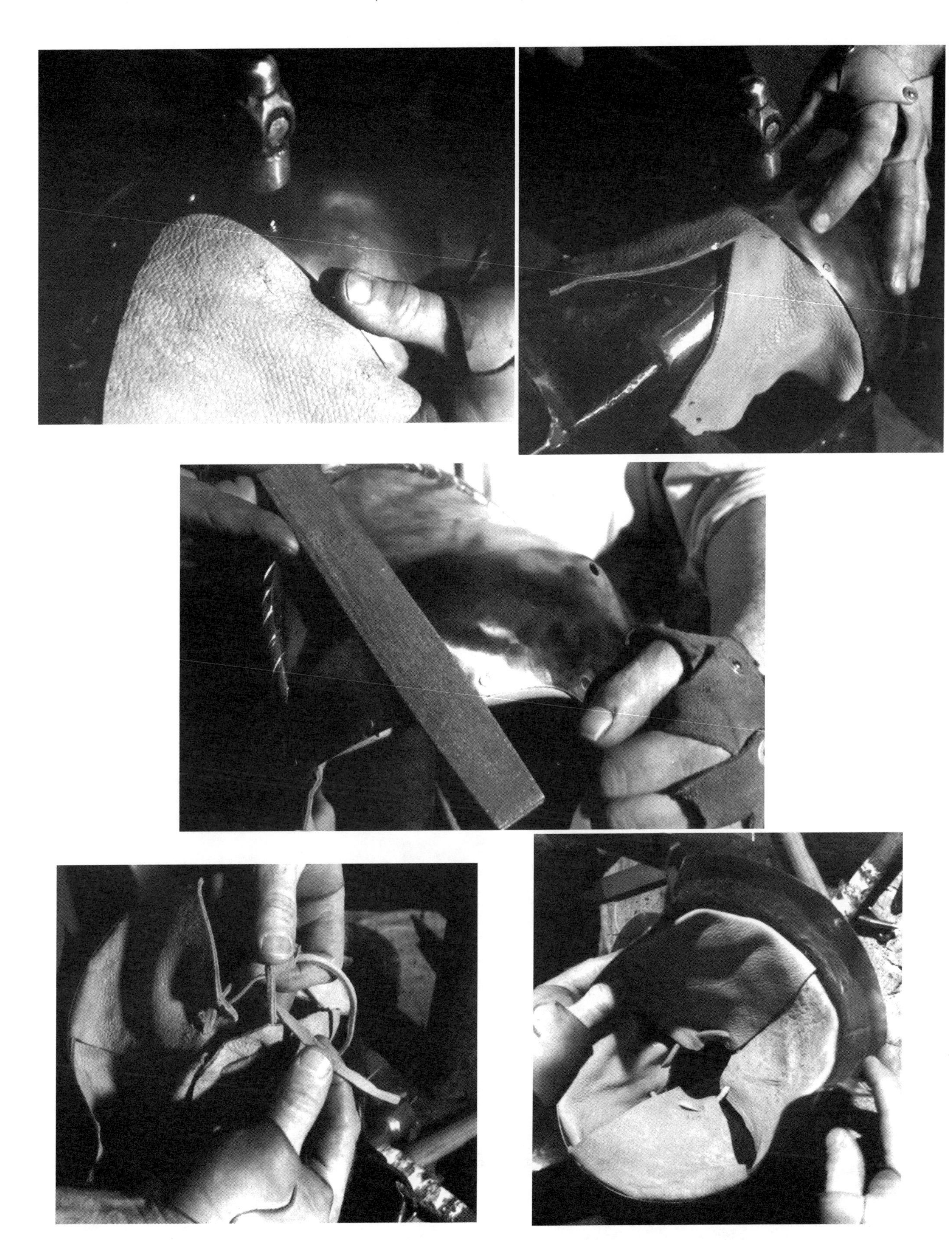

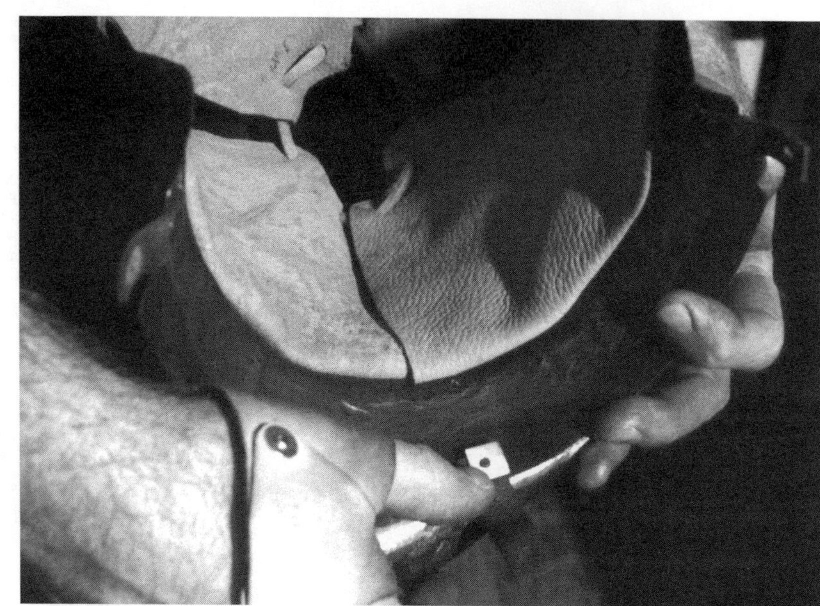

The gorget plate is attached at the back of the helmet.

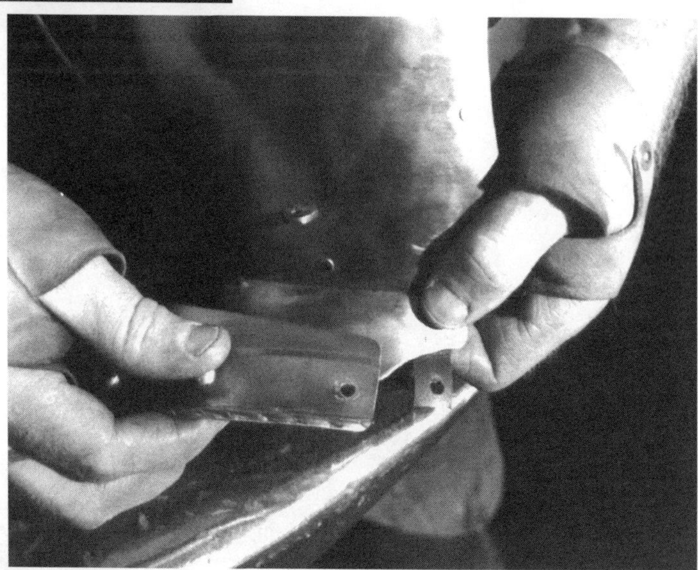

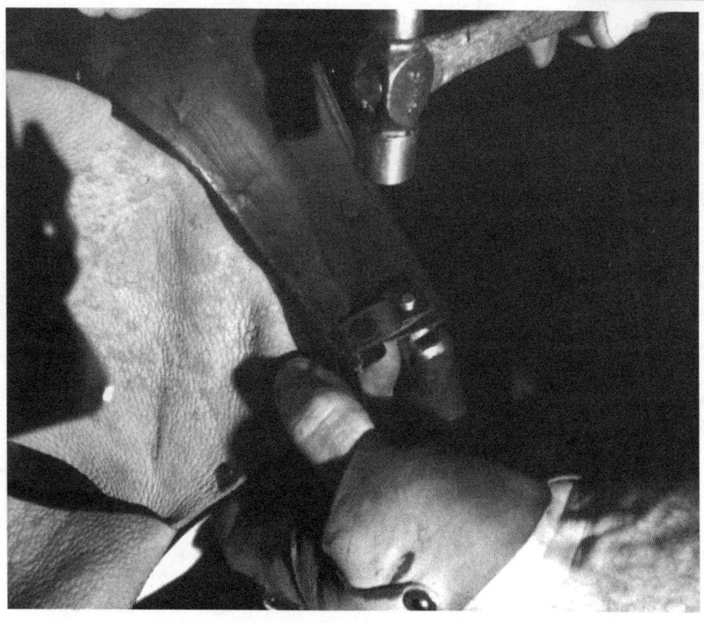

Both halves are attached with the pivoting nuts and bolts, shown here with the locking hook to keep the helmet together.

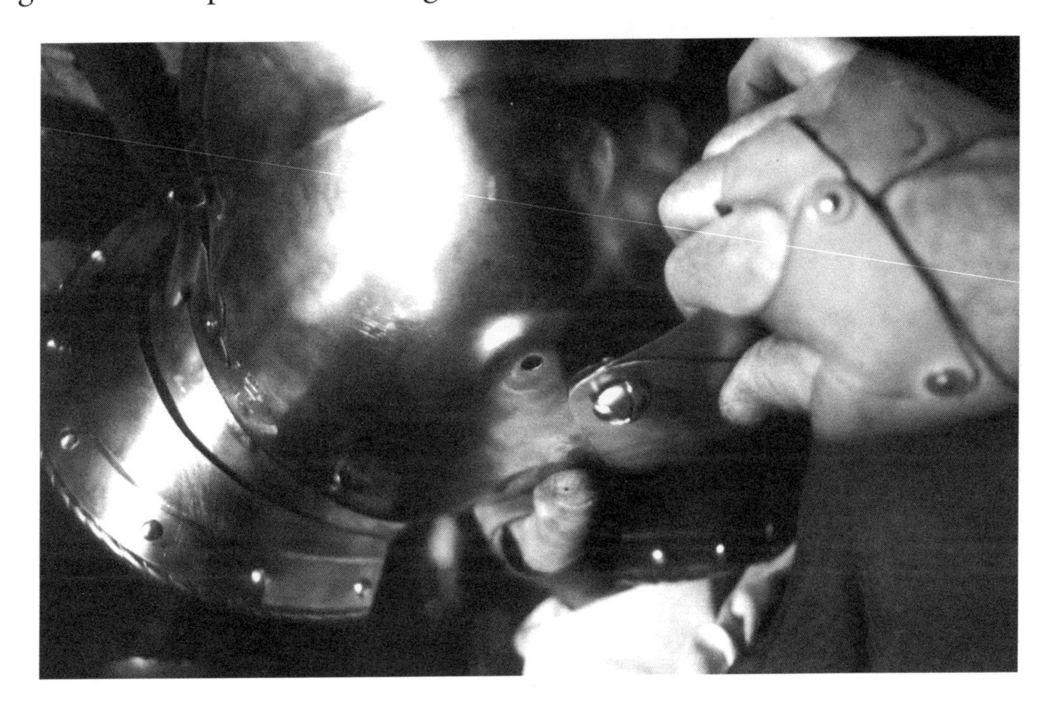

Historically, it was the armourer's apprentice who polished armour pieces by hand or on large polishing wheels driven by water wheels. We demonstrate this by hand, using a similar compound of linseed oil and fine sand, called pumice.

When pieces were polished, they were ready to try on.

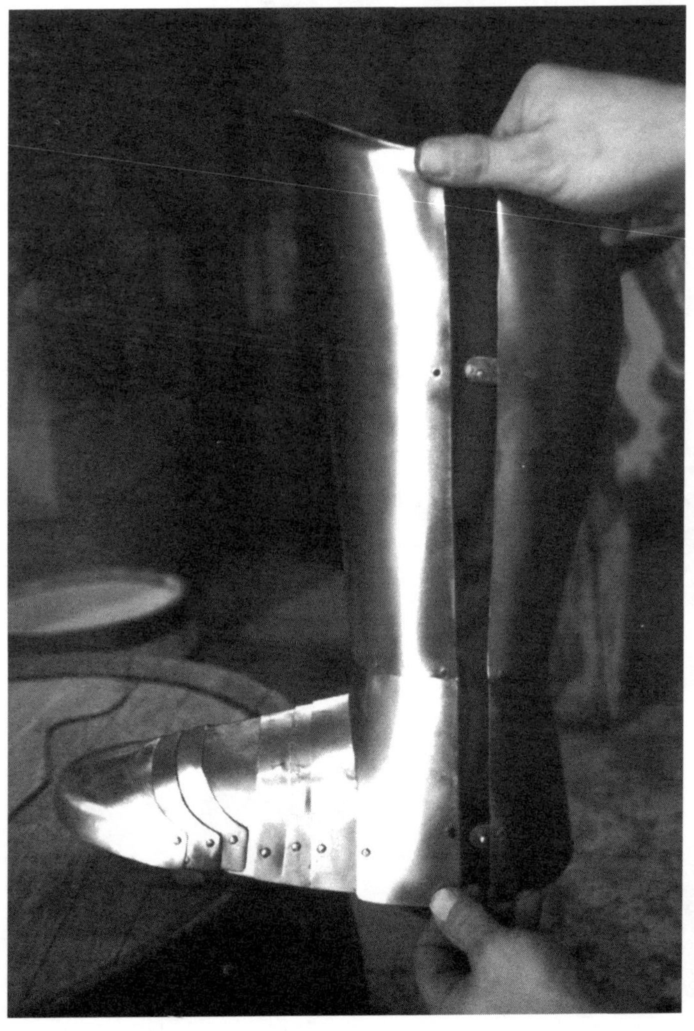

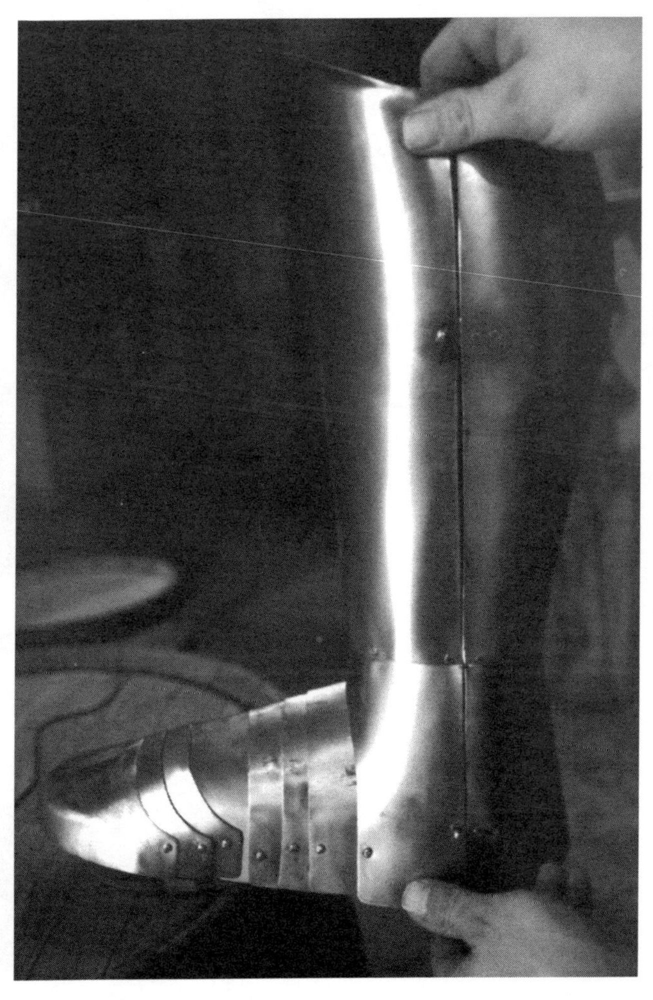

Armour most often required assistance to don. Usually a knight would have one particular squire that was in charge of this armour, and would assist with putting the armour on his knight. Here the customer tries on his new armour for the first time.

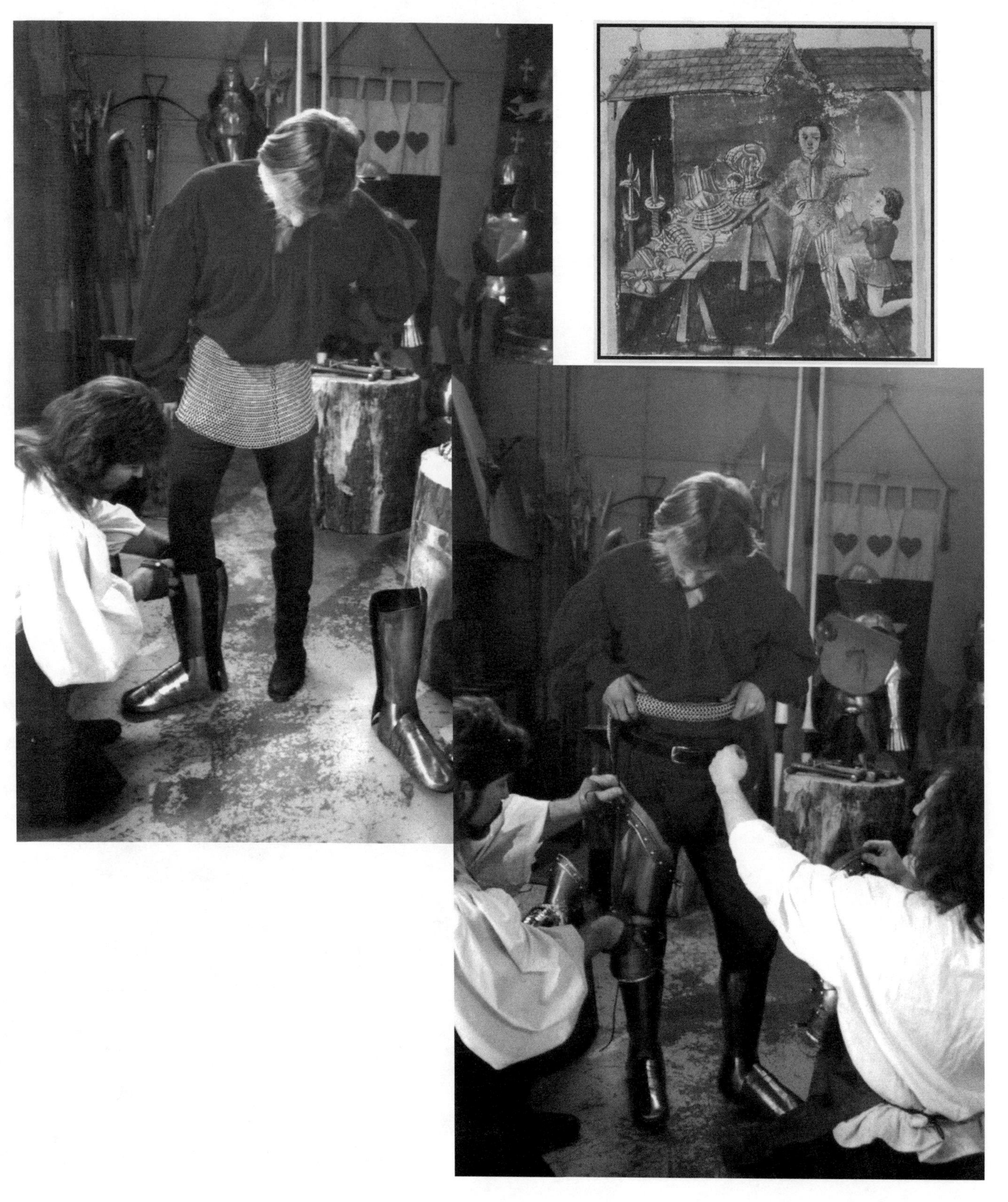

Armour is put on from the feet up. The legs are suspended by a belt under the chainmail skirt.

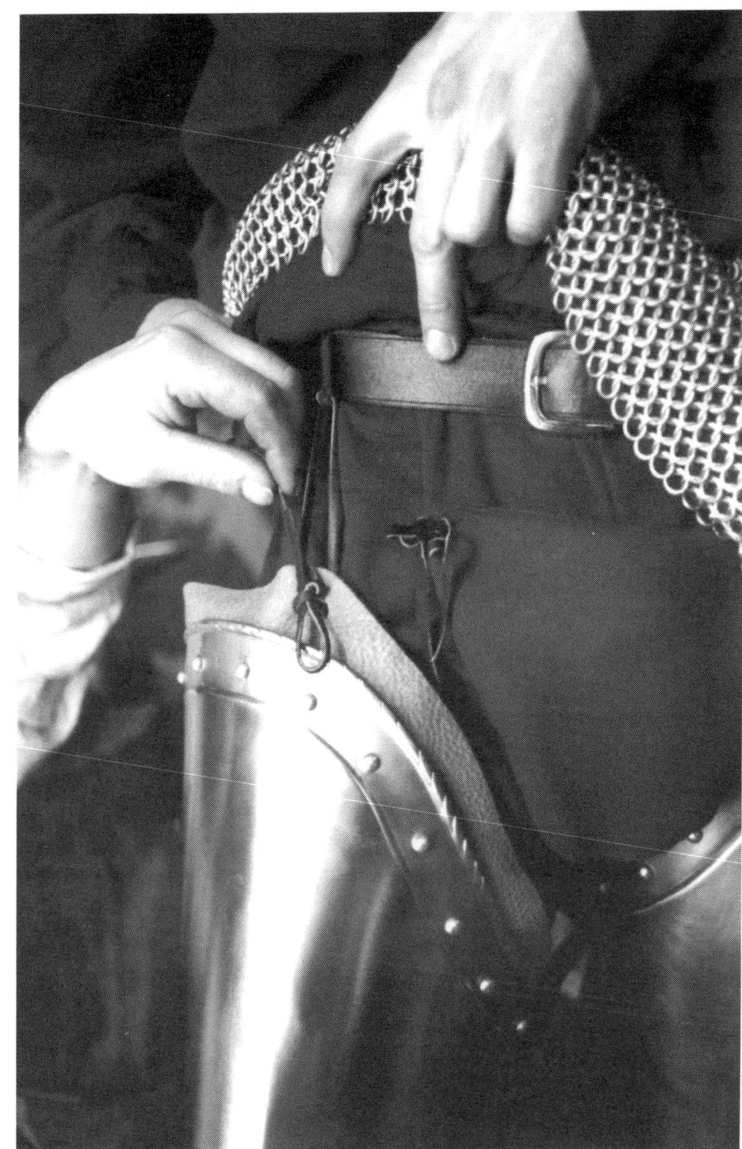

The gorget is worn under the breast and back plates, so it is put on next.

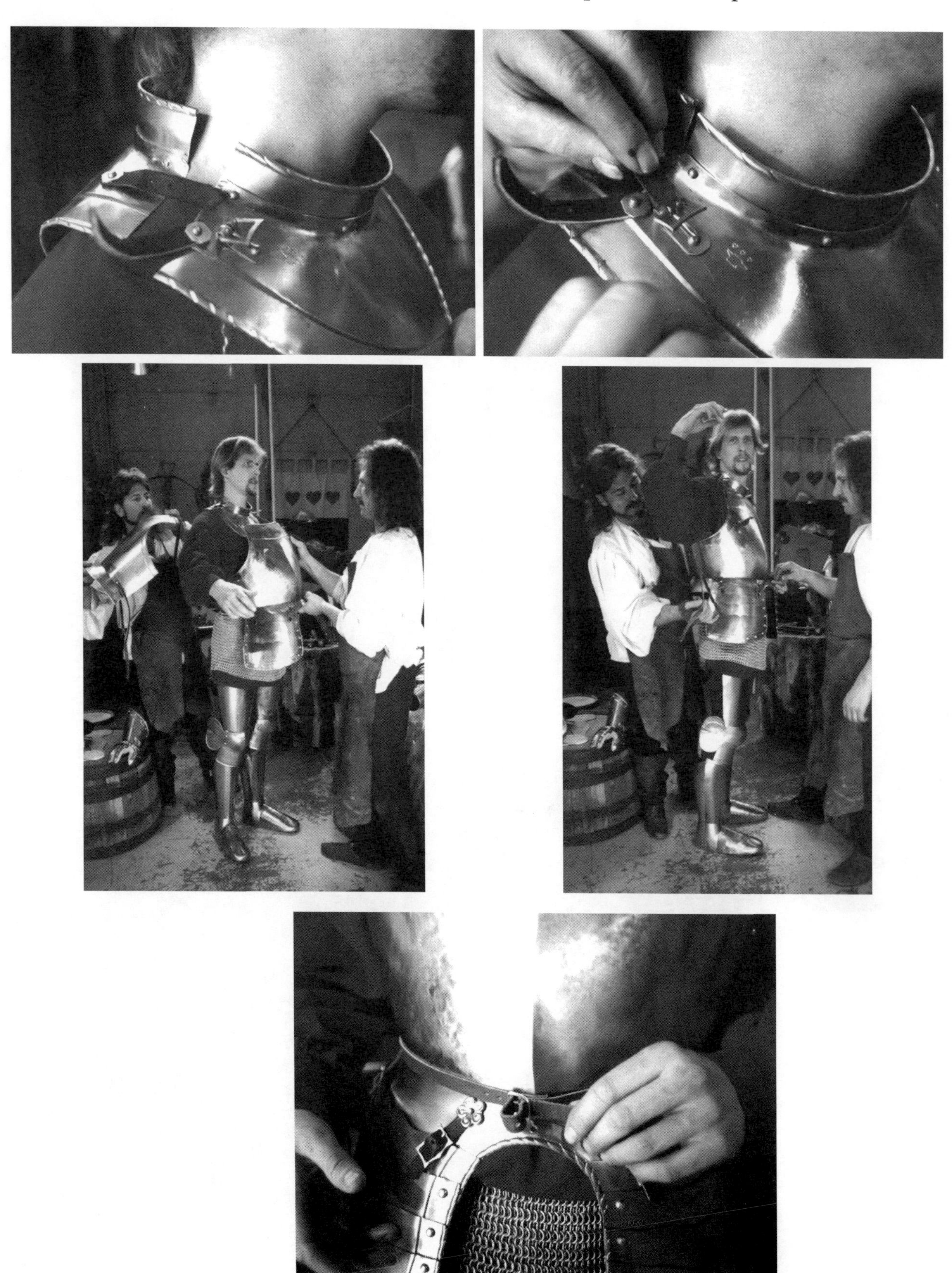

Next, the arm harnesses are attached. These are suspended by buckles, but often are connected by a steel spring pin.

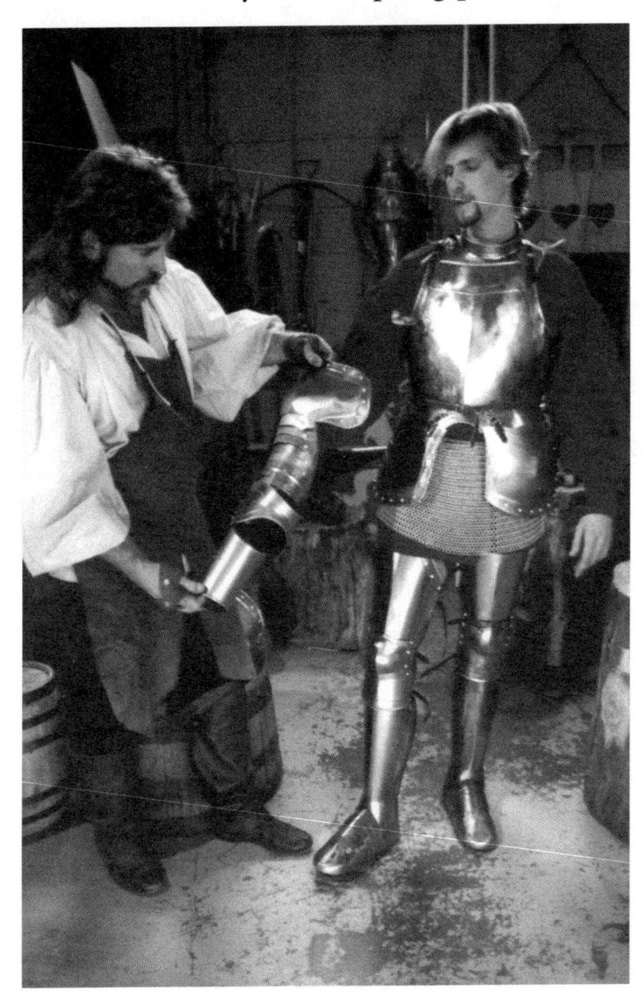

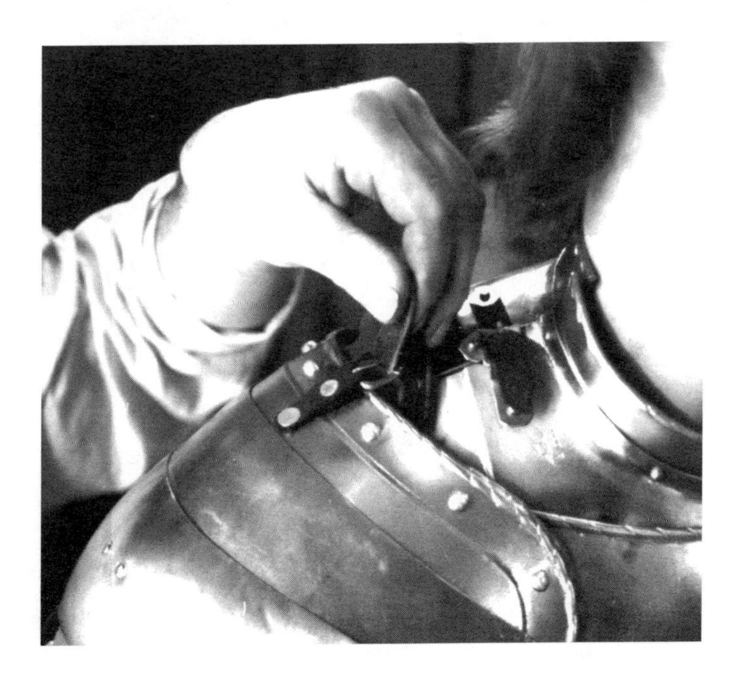

The vambraces have lock pins.

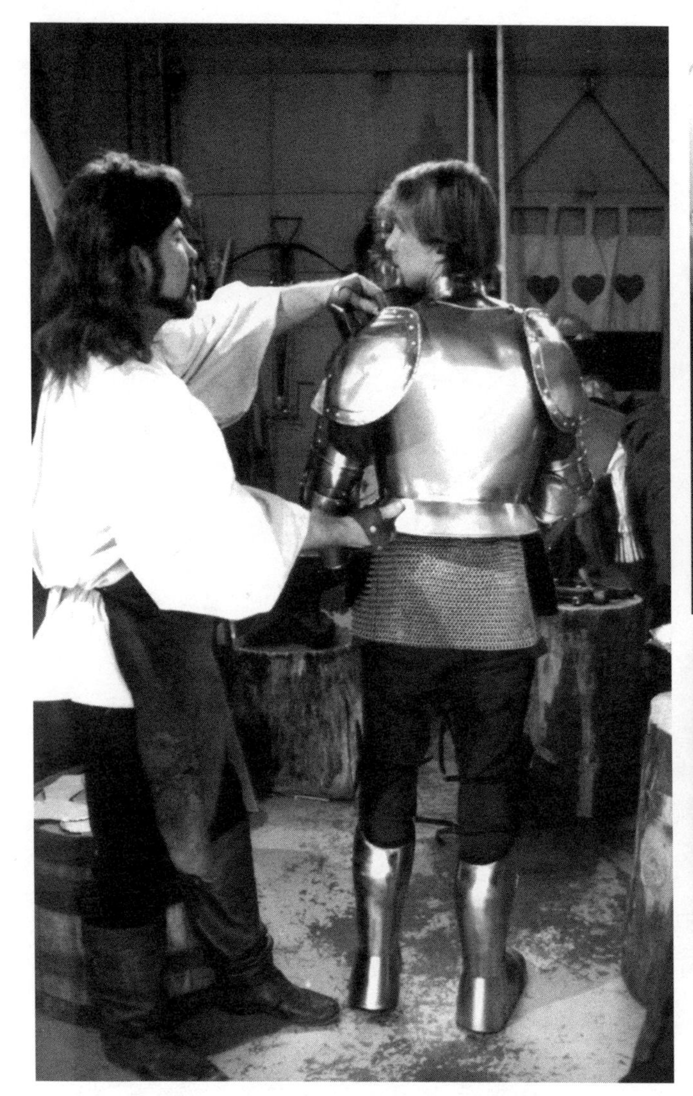

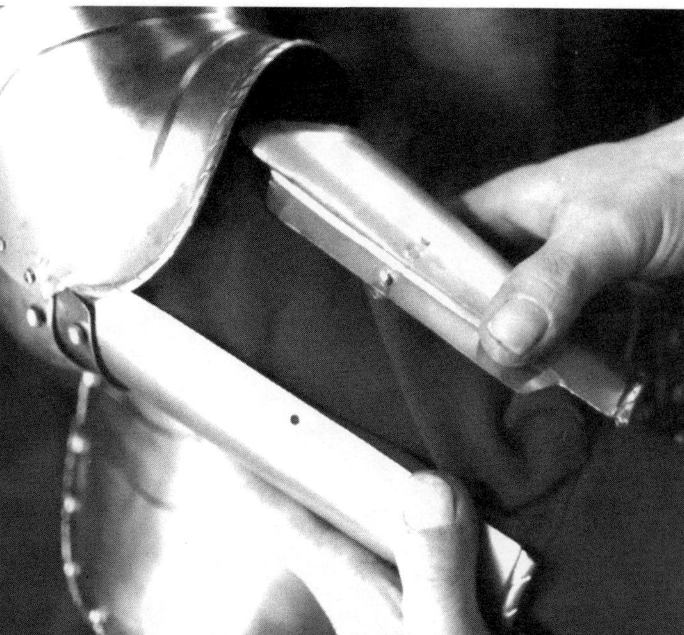

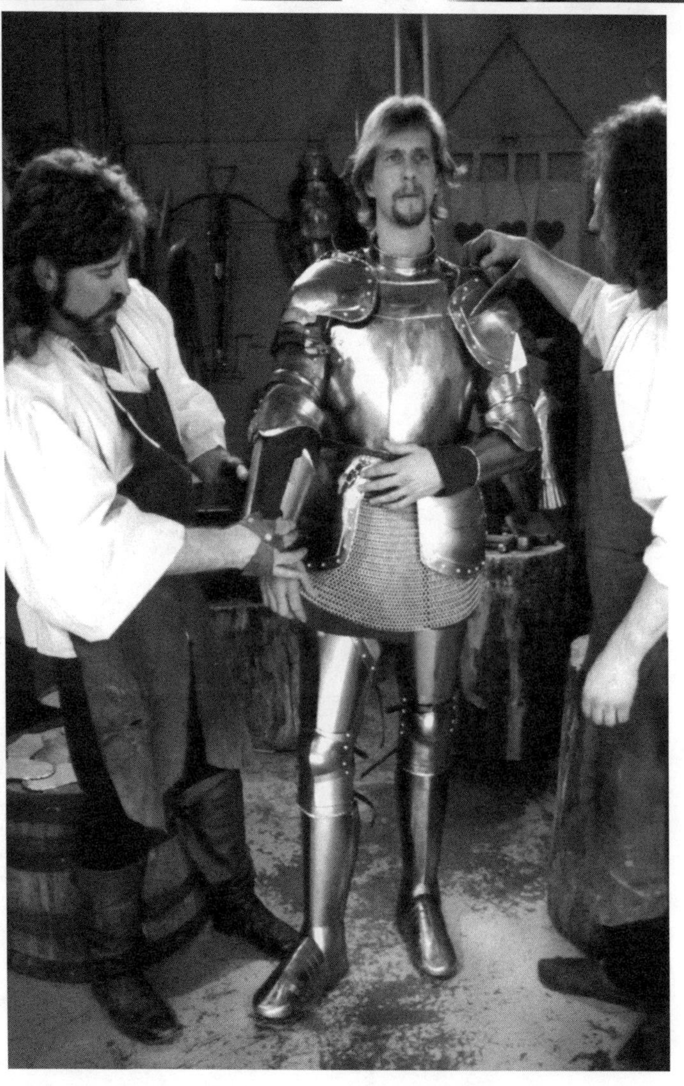

Next the helmet goes on. Note the absence of holes on the left side of the ventail, this is to give it a better glancing surface for any weapon or projectile. Usual blows would come from the right hand and land on the left side of the knight.

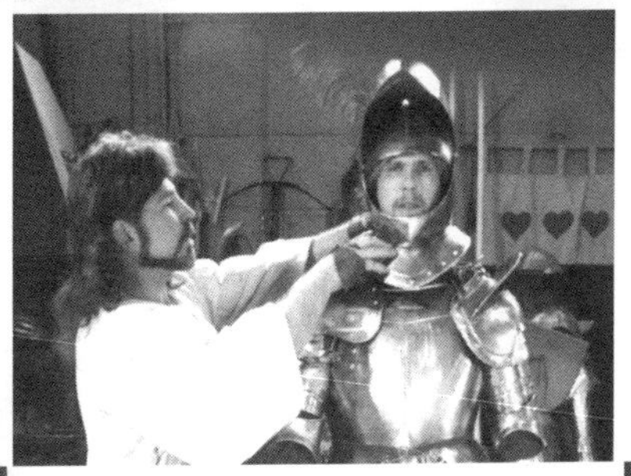

The final piece of armour to be put on are the gauntlets. The customer then tries moving in the complete suit to see if it binds anywhere. He gets final adjustments made to the suit.

He tries a sword out as well as a lance.

If a knight could afford armour, he most definitely owned several horses, and most full armour was designed to be worn on horseback. He would be the pinnacle in battlefield weaponry, and very well protected.